the yogurt
cookbook

*For my mother, Camilla Schulz, who
always had quark in her fridge.
For Arto Der Harountunian: it was an
honor to photograph your recipes;
I wish we could have cooked together.
For Michel Moushabeck who inspired my
photography. And for all of you: I invite
you to try these sumptuous dishes.*
—H. S.

the yogurt cookbook

arto der haroutunian

photography by hiltrud schulz

Interlink Books

AN IMPRINT OF INTERLINK PUBLISHING GROUP, INC.

NORTHAMPTON, MASSACHUSETTS

ACKNOWLEDGEMENTS
I would like to thank Jenny Daniell, Holly Fisher, James McDonald, Leyla Moushabeck,
Samar Moushabeck and Marta Ostapiuk for lending me props for the photo shoot.
Thanks also to Ramzi Moushabeck and Marta Ostapiuk for their help with the cooking.
And thanks to all of my friends for testing the recipes and eating the food.

First illustrated edition published in 2013 by
INTERLINK BOOKS
An imprint of Interlink Publishing Group, Inc.
46 Crosby Street, Northampton, MA 01060
www.interlinkbooks.com

General Editor: Michel S. Moushabeck
Editors: Leyla Moushabeck, Sara Rauch
Food and Prop Stylist: Hiltrud Schulz
Proofreader: Jennifer M. Staltare, Mora Couch
Production: Pam Fontes-May
Photography: Hiltrud Schulz
Photo Editor: Hannah Moushabeck
Book Design: James McDonald, The Impress Group

Library of Congress Cataloging-in-Publication Data

Der Haroutunian, Arto, 1940-1987
The yogurt cookbook / by Arto Der Haroutunian. -- 1st American ed.
p. cm.   Includes index.   ISBN 978-1-56656-861-6 (hardcover)
1. Cooking (Yogurt) I. Title.
TX759.5.Y63D47 2012   641.6'71476--dc23   2012014827

Printed and bound in China

contents

introduction

I owe my family and age to yogurt, nothing else—not even God!

—M. Husseynov at the age of 147

When my family emigrated to Britain in the 1950s with all our domestic paraphernalia including pots and pans, thick woollen blankets, a large packet of Turkish coffee, some dried eggplant, zucchini, and okra—vegetables unheard of by the British public in those days—as well as old personal relics, my mother brought with her in her handbag a small jar of yogurt which, she proudly announced, was to be the "starter" for the new bowl of yogurt she intended to make on our arrival. The starter of that same jar had been brought over from the "old country"—Armenia, where my family originated—years before and, no doubt in some form or other, had been in our family for generations. Talk about eternity! Indeed, what I really should have said at the start is that yogurt begets yogurt; it is eternal. Let me explain.

The Russian-born French bacteriologist Dr. Illya Metchnikov (1845–1916), director of the Pasteur Institute in Paris and, in 1908, co-winner of the Nobel Prize for physiology and medicine (for his work on the infection-fighting properties of white blood cells) carried out a great deal of his research in the Balkans among the Bulgarian peasantry who, though extremely impoverished, had an average life expectancy of eighty-seven years. He concluded that this remarkable longevity was partly due to a drink called yogurt. In his laboratory he isolated the two types of bacilli (*Lactobacillus bulgaricus* and *Streptococcus thermophilus*) that are responsible for changing milk to yogurt. Metchnikov proved scientifically what Middle Eastern people had known for centuries that yogurt—a fermented, slightly acidic, semi-solid cultured milk related to other fermented milks—arrested internal putrefaction, has antibiotic properties that restore normal intestinal equilibrium, and is excellent for the aged, the young, and people with weak digestion. Yogurt contains a higher percentage of lactic acid $C_3H_6O_3$, the acid formed in milk, than other fermented milks and is very rich in vitamin B2 complex. It has no more calories than milk. The yogurt culture remains alive even after the passage through the intestine whereas the bacillus of other milk products is destroyed.

In the Caucasus, people have believed in the healing power of yogurt for centuries. They have attributed their longevity to it and have maintained, for example, that yogurt with garlic is an excellent cure for tuberculosis, that it helps dysentery, averts a hangover, increases sexual potency, and even remedies baldness!

I remember that as a child I came to detest that thick, white, jelly-like food simply because I was forced to eat it day in, day out, on its own, with honey, as a salad or a drink, in stews or soups. Now, however, with the accumulation of gray hair and creeping middle age I have come to see not only its many benefits but I have come to like it so much that, like a born-again believer, I have compiled this book of recipes to demonstrate how versatile and exciting yogurt can be.

The name "yogurt" is said to be either Bulgarian or Turkish in origin. This is not so. It is Armenian and derives from two Indo-European roots—*yough* (oil) and gurd (curd; *guard* in Armenian). Thus *yough-guard* means the oil of the curd, i.e. the whey. *Masta* on the other hand means curdled milk in Sanskrit. This has been passed into Persian and Kurdish as *mast* and into Armenian as *madz-oon*. In Armenian *ma-guard* is the bacillus, i.e. the curd of *masta*. Thus the word yogurt is derived from the word for whey, and not the word for curd. For the sake of accuracy we should call yogurt either *masta* or *mast* or *madzoon*. We must also remember that while the above languages are Indo-European and the people Indo-Aryan by origin, both the Bulgarian and Turkish people, in language and origin, are of Mongolian stock, with a language that belongs to the Altaic family.

There are many fanciful and semi-mythological stories on the origin of yogurt. Here are a few for interest.

The Tajik and Mongolian nomadic tribes carried their milk in gourds strung over the backs of camels. Sunshine and the constant jolting turned it thick and sour.

Early Greeks and desert nomads used to have their goats' and sheep's milk exposed to the bacteria of the open air and thus it developed a new character.

Finally, the best of all, when Noah's Ark was floating over the waves and the animals produced all that milk poor old Noah had nowhere to store it and so he used sewn-up bags made of animal stomach and, to his great surprise, one day he found that the milk had thickened. At first he thought "what a waste," but when he tried it he liked the flavor and thus yogurt was born. However fanciful this last explanation is, it is very probably nearest to the truth, for the lining of a calf's stomach contains an enzyme, rennin, which produces rennet—the curdling agent.

Around about 10,000 BC the Aryan tribes made their appearances in eastern Turkey, northern Iran, and the northwest of India. They left a great religious compendium known as the "Vedas," the most important of which is the *Rig Veda*, written over three thousand years ago. It reflects the religious beliefs, the customs, and thoughts of the people who wrote it. Agriculture was the main activity of the Aryans. They tilled the soil with ploughs pulled by oxen—a custom that still persists in Turkey, Iran, and India. The Aryans' herds were one of their main sources of wealth. The cow, which provided milk, was held in great esteem—as it still is in India. Milk and butter were the staple foods of the Aryans and were offered as libations to the gods. The Aryans also ate meat. They were great hunters, killing their game with bows and arrows or using ingenious traps. They grilled the meat on open fires.

Agri was the god of the fire, and he engendered the other gods. *Soma* or *homa*—the ambrosia of the other races—was the fermented liquid that gave force to Agri, made the gods immortal, and filled the men with vigor. I believe this was none other than *masta* (yogurt), to which was added the plant *homa* (*Sarcostema vininelis*). The result, a strong, intoxicating brew, which was considered healthy, nutritious, and capable of providing strength as well as prolonging life, was truly the food of the gods! Indeed, among the Yogis, yogurt mixed with honey is still considered a food of the gods; it is the name of the ancient Zoroastrian supreme deity Ahura-Masta (Ara-mast in Armenian), meaning "all-powerful *masta*," clearly reflects the great importance the Aryan tribes attributed to curdled milk.

There is no doubt that yogurt and yogurt-based dishes have played an important role in the diet of the Aryan races. However it did not remain their prerogative for long; its existence and uses were, in time, passed on to other people. References to yogurt and other curdled milks abound in the written records of ancient civilizations. The Egyptians and Israelites favored it. The Greeks were aware of its healthful properties and the historians Herodotus and Pliny the Elder wrote about cultured milks.

Throughout the ages, conquering races—Arabs and then Turks—helped to spread yogurt from its "homeland" (i.e. the area of the Middle East that today comprises the states of Turkey, Armenia, Kurdistan, and most of Iran) to the neighboring lands as far as Romania in the west and India in the east. From the Aryan Persians, the Arabs acquired the knowledge of rice, tea, and yogurt, which they called *Halib-el-Ajam* (Persian milk). The Persians also spread its popularity throughout Afghanistan, northern India, and Pakistan. Interestingly enough there is no yogurt today in China, Japan, Korea, Mongolia, nor even in most of central Asia. Yogurt is known in northern Egypt, but is not popular. It is little used in North African cuisine and the yogurt eaten in Ethiopia, Sudan, and Somalia is more of a curdled milk than a true yogurt.

For centuries, there has been controversy in the Middle East between peoples—especially Greeks and Turks—about the origin of certain dishes. One claims all is really his, the other screams "*Yok*"—No! As with everything in life, nothing belongs to one man. Food varies, it is developed and adapted in response to economic and cultural pressure. All that man has created or, should I say adapted from nature, is man's. The name may change, he may favor one or other ingredient, but in essence the product is the same—nature's.

For centuries the people of the Middle East, by whatever name they are known, have used yogurt. Today it has broken through to the West, has gained respectability and become one of the "in" things; worshipped by the nature-food lovers, clinically approved by the scientists, and tolerated by the *haute cuisine* priests. The introduction of yogurt into western Europe is attributed to the French king François I, after he had been cured by an Armenian healer from Constantinople who, arriving on foot with a herd of goats, prepared (in great secrecy) a batch of yogurt and prescribed it to the monarch, restored his health and returned home—presumably still on foot! Despite a few pockets of devotees (Armenian, Jewish, and Greek merchants) and some flurries of interest down through the centuries, nobody in the West even knew or cared about yogurt—until Metchnikov. After his death a Spaniard named Issac Carasso opened the first modern yogurt plants in Barcelona and Paris. During and after the Second World War the Carasso family business opened other factories in the USA and France, marketing their product under the brand name of "Dannon" ("Danone" in France). The first commercially produced yogurt in the USA was sold under the name of "Madzoon" in the early 1920s. In 1929 the Colombosian family, Armenian immigrants, introduced a whole-milk yogurt, "Colombo," which was especially popular on the east coast of the USA, while the Kazanis family sold their product under the label of "Oxyzala." In Britain in the early 1930s "Yegvart's Yogurt" was highly popular in the northwest.

These early pioneering families were Middle Easterners and, indeed, it could not have been otherwise for, just as with my own mother, many other Middle

Eastern women brought over with them to the West a jar or two of the "food of the gods" as an inherent part of their culture and traditions. The first reported appearance of yogurt in the Americas was 1784 when Armenian and Greek immigrants, fleeing the harsh Ottoman misrule, brought with them the dried yogurt culture and prepared their favorite food as they had back in the "old country."

Today, yogurt is big business, with several major concerns fighting for ever-increasing markets and offering the consumer a vast choice—natural yogurt, fruit yogurt, sweetened yogurt, and frozen yogurt. It was decided by early manufacturers that yogurt should be given a new look. Therefore the first step was to prepare it with partially skimmed milk thus reducing the calorie content without affecting the nutritive value. In contrast the Middle Eastern and most homemade versions tend to be very rich and creamy with a tart flavor as they are made with whole milk. The next step was to remove the tart flavor of plain yogurt by sweetening it. This was done by adding fruit preserves and flavors. Indeed, the sweetening of yogurt was the prime reason for its sudden popularity throughout the West, where it is still consumed primarily as a snack or dessert.

But yogurt is more than a dessert. Its versatility has been known for centuries by the people of the Middle East, Caucasus, the Balkans, and India where it appears in soups, salads, sauces, stews, pastries, and sweets, enhancing and enriching the food, giving it flavor and a touch of magic. In the West most people do not know of the many uses of yogurt, hence this book, which I hope will be the "starter" for your experiments with this many-faceted ingredient worthy of the gods! With yogurt, almost anything goes. The possibilities of cooking with it are infinite. It is a good substitute for cream, milk, buttermilk, and sour cream. It makes an excellent marinade, and goes well with vegetables, eggs, meat, poultry, cheese, and grains.

In this book I have collected recipes from all over the land where yogurt has always been used. Most are very old, some relatively new, and a few are adaptations of old recipes where I suggest yogurt was once used—or should have been. My sources are varied—ancient manuscripts, old cookbooks, a poem or two, friends, relations, relations of friends, and friends of relations. I have found one book on yogurt by Irfan Orga, *Cooking with Yogurt* (Andre Deutsch, 1956), which I have consulted with pleasure. Some of the recipes have been eye-openers to me and I have included a few in my collection.

My advice is first to use these recipes and then to make up your own, thus enriching not only your taste and plate, but the use of yogurt.

I believe that of all the Middle Eastern ingredients and forms of cooking, yogurt is by far the most exciting, not only in what it already offers, but because there are countless variations and new uses will continue to be discovered in the years to come.

QUANTITIES

All the recipes are for four people, unless otherwise indicated.

METRICATION

I have not always used exact equivalents for quantities in the metric and the customary US units. I have tried to make the measurements in both systems easily workable, while keeping the proportions right. It is therefore important when using the recipes to stick to either one or the other—try not to switch between the two.

SPOONS

Where quantities are measured in teaspoons or tablespoons use a *level* spoonful.

GLOSSARY

There is a glossary of the less familiar ingredients on pp. 296–297.

how to make yogurt

how to make yogurt

basic yogurt recipes

basic data

BACTERIA

Yogurt is made with a culture containing the beneficial bacteria (*Lactobacillus bulgaricus* and *Streptococcus thermophilus*), which are allowed to multiply freely in milk at a controlled temperature until it achieves the proper semi-solid consistency and tart flavor. The bacteria are rich in B vitamins—excellent for maintaining a healthy intestinal system.

CONTENTS

1 cup (225 ml) of plain yogurt made from 2% milk contains:

89 percent water	294mg calcium
125 calories	1mg iron
8g protein	170 units vitamin A
4g fat	10mg thiamine
13g carbohydrate	44mg riboflavin
	2mg niacin
	2mg ascorbic acid

Yogurt is a particularly good source of calcium.

FREEZING

Do not freeze as freezing and thawing adversely affect the smooth texture.

REFRIGERATION

Homemade yogurt should be refrigerated in order to halt any further growth of bacteria. It will then keep for up to a week before it starts to become too acidic. Commercial yogurt should be refrigerated immediately after purchase and should be consumed within three to four days—otherwise the acidity will continue to increase and so a sharper flavor will be produced.

WHEY

This is the watery part of the milk that separates from the curds after coagulation. This is the real yogurt (see p. 7). It is used extensively in Iranian and Indian cuisine.

yogurt makes yogurt

Just a little yogurt—about one teaspoon per 2 cups (½ l) of milk—when put into warm milk will make more yogurt. How? Because it is its own bacillus, or starter.

Any commercial natural yogurt can be used as a starter and thereafter your own yogurt will supply the bacillus needed. There are several methods of yogurt preparation. Here is the simple, age-old method handed down from generation to generation—in my opinion, the best.

4 cups (1 l) milk
1 tablespoon yogurt as a starter

1. Bring the milk to a boil in a saucepan.
2. When the froth rises turn off the heat.
3. Allow the milk to cool to the point where you can dip your finger in and count up to fifteen—without screaming! This is to ascertain that the correct temperature has been reached. As we are dealing with living bacteria it is essential that the temperature is kept between 120°F (49°C), above which it will be killed, and 90°F (32°C), below which it will not grow. Use a thermometer if you do not trust your finger.
4. Remove the skin that has formed on the surface of the milk. (This is the cream. Let it cool, add some sugar to it, and eat it spread on a piece of bread.

I rate this as one of the great luxuries of life! This cream is called *ser* or *kaymak* and is highly prized throughout the Middle East, where it is made very thick and is consumed for breakfast. It is also a basic ingredient of many desserts.)

5. Beat the yogurt (starter) in a cup, add a tablespoon of the warm milk, beat vigorously, and pour into the rest of the milk.
6. Empty the milk into an earthenware or glass bowl and stir a few times.
7. Cover the bowl with a large plate and wrap in a dish towel.
8. Put in a warm, dry place (e.g. near a radiator or fireplace) and do not disturb for 8 to 10 hours.

Yogurt can be kept for up to a week in the fridge. When it is nearly finished make a new batch by using a little starter from the previous batch.

Homemade yogurt is not only cheaper than store-bought, it is also much nicer because it is less acidic—yogurt gets sourer with age—and is lighter in texture.

THE OPTIMISTIC APPROACH

This recipe reminds me of a would-be great entrepreneur who was seen seated at the seaside pouring yogurt out of large cups into water and then stirring it vigorously with a large wooden spoon.

A friend passed by and asked, "What are you doing?"

"Making yogurt."

"You're joking. How can you make yogurt? It is impossible, it couldn't possibly hold. I mean, it's water, not milk!"

"Yes, I agree the chance of it working is very slim, but just visualize if it does . . . I mean, just think of the fortune to be made."

The friend is stunned, amazed, mesmerized.

"Here, let me give you a hand."

"No thanks, I'll tell you what you can do."

"What?"

"Go and buy a ton of cucumber and we'll have a sea full of *jajig*."

"A wonderful idea." The friend rushes off to the market.

"Don't bother with the salt," the entrepreneur shouts after him, "it's already salted."

ALTERNATIVE METHODS OF MAKING YOGURT

There are many different kinds of yogurt-making equipment available today. They all work well. Some electric yogurt makers are fairly expensive, but they make the process completely effortless, as you need not heat the milk or use a thermometer. The machine does all the work.

Another method involves using an insulated jar or thermos. This method makes good yogurt but has one drawback: after the setting time you should decant the yogurt into a bowl to chill otherwise it over-incubates and becomes too acidic. Personally I prefer to stick to the tried and true method.

A FEW FURTHER HINTS

1. Use absolutely clean, well-rinsed utensils and containers.
2. If you use sterilized milk rather than pasteurized it is not necessary to bring it to a boil first. Simply heat it to the required temperature (110°F/43°C).
3. If you are dieting, use skim milk instead of whole milk.
4. If there is no yogurt starter or bacillus available you can use dried powder culture, which can be bought from health stores or online.
5. If you want a thicker, creamier yogurt, stir skim milk powder into the milk at the outset—1 teaspoon for every 2 cups (½ L) milk.

REGULATING THE TASTE

The taste of homemade yogurt can be regulated. For a mild flavor, chill as soon as the yogurt begins to thicken. For a stronger flavor, incubate it for a longer period.

REASONS FOR FAILURE

You may find that occasionally your yogurt will not set and will separate instead into curds and whey. The main causes of this are:

1. The milk was not at the right temperature, i.e. between 90°F (32°C) and 120°F (49°C), when the starter was added.
2. The incubation temperature was either too low or too high.

3. The wrong amount of starter was added. Either too much or too little will cause it to separate.

FLAVORS

If you wish to flavor your yogurt, it is best to do so after it has thickened. It is much easier to achieve the actual taste you require and it prevents the flavoring from sinking, which it tends to do—especially if you are using pieces of fruit.

STABILIZING YOGURT

If you are going to use yogurt in a recipe that involves boiling it, it is necessary to stabilize it first or it will separate and appear lumpy. This will not actually affect the taste, but will simply make the dish a little less attractive. If you cannot eat all the fresh yogurt you have before it becomes too acidic, then stabilize it and use it for cooking.

To stabilize the yogurt *EITHER* stir 1 to 2 teaspoons flour into a little water and then add to the yogurt before cooking, *OR* beat an egg into the yogurt before cooking. Note that once yogurt has been stabilized and boiled it cannot be used as a starter, as the bacteria die at high temperatures.

labna

YOGURT CHEESE

This appetizer is a must on any Syrian or Lebanese breakfast table, where it is consumed with hot pita bread.

1. Make the yogurt (see p. 14). I suggest you try making *labna* with 2 cups (½ l) of yogurt first. You can increase the quantity later if you find that you like it and are going to consume it in vast quantities!
2. *Either* line a colander with a piece of damp muslin, *or* sew a muslin or loosely woven cotton bag with a drawstring top about 12 x 12 in (30 x 30 cm) in size.
3. Spoon the yogurt into the colander or bag and leave to drain for 5 to 6 hours in the sink (or suspend the bag over a bowl). The whey will drain away leaving a light, soft, creamy cheese.
4. Serve it on a small plate, sprinkled with a little dried mint or some other herb (chopped dill, parsley, chives, tarragon) or with a little olive oil poured over the top.
5. Decorate with a pinch of paprika and a few black olives. Serve it for breakfast or as an hors d'oeuvre.

dahi, urgo

Dahi is the Indian name for yogurt and *urgo* is the Ethiopian. Both are names for the same thing, but it is not yogurt as we know it. It is, in reality, milk curdled with the addition of a few drops of lemon juice and stirred continuously until the milk has completely curdled. The milk is covered and left for 15 to 20 minutes and then the curds are strained from the whey. (Turkish peasants sometimes squeeze in a few drops of fresh fig juice to curdle the milk.)

The Ethiopians and other neighboring nationalities consume a great deal of *urgo*. Since their diet consists basically of a sour spongy bread called *injera*—made of *teff* flour—and generally hot and spicy food, *urgo* is the ideal accompaniment. It is almost always served with meals, both at home and in restaurants.

It will not act as a bacillus or starter, but it makes excellent cottage cheese.

madzna banir

YOGURT CHEESE

A charming and simple Armenian hors d'oeuvre. *Labna* (see previous page) is shaped into small balls, drenched in olive oil, and then sprinkled with fresh herbs. Serve as an appetizer with *lavash* or pita bread and a glass of arak (or any favorite aperitif).

4 cups (1 l) yogurt
1 teaspoon salt
scant ½ cup (100 ml) olive oil
1 tablespoon chopped fresh mint
1 tablespoon chopped fresh dill

2 tablespoons finely chopped scallions
1 tablespoon finely chopped fresh chives

1. Mix the yogurt and salt and drain as for *labna*, p. 18.
2. Spoon the thickened yogurt into a bowl and then shape into walnut-sized balls.
3. Arrange the balls on a large serving plate and pour the olive oil over them.
4. Mix all the herbs together in a bowl and then sprinkle them over the balls.

panir

INDIAN FRESH CHEESE

Panir in Hindi, *panir* and *banir* in Farsi and Armenian, and *beynir* in Turkish all refer to the same thing—fresh cheese made from milk. It is extensively used in both savory and sweet dishes and is a less sophisticated form of *labna* or *chortan*. It is used in such dishes as *matar panir* (peas with fresh cheese, see p. 128) and many other vegetable dishes where, as well as adding extra nutrition, it helps balance the strong, spicy flavors of most Indian dishes. There is a recipe for *ras gula* (*panir* in syrup) in the section dealing with sweets (p. 259).

6 cups (1½ l) milk

1 tablespoon lemon juice

1. Bring the milk to a boil in a saucepan, stirring from time to time to prevent a skin forming.
2. Remove from the heat and gradually add the lemon juice, stirring continuously until the milk has curdled completely.
3. Cover and set aside for 15 to 20 minutes.
4. Strain through a muslin cloth to ensure that all the watery whey is removed.
5. Wrap the loose curds—*chenna* in Hindi— in the cloth, and compress with a weight for 2 to 3 hours.
6. The cheese can then be stored in the refrigerator and cut into cubes whenever needed.

chortan

DRIED YOGURT BALLS

In ancient times and in some villages even today, Armenian women used to make yogurt, then strain it, dry it in the sun, and store it to use at any time of year in soups. In Iran, this is known as *kashk* and in Afghanistan, it is called *kurut*.

1. Prepare the *labna* (see p. 18).
2. Knead it well.
3. Make it into walnut-sized balls.
4. Arrange the balls on a tray and dry. Traditionally this would be done in the sun, but can also be achieved by placing the balls in a warm, dry place for about 48 hours and then left in the oven at the lowest temperature for 24 hours. It is not the same as sun-drying but it is the nearest substitute.
5. When the *chortan* balls are thoroughly dry they should be as hard as stone.
6. Store them in an airtight jar and use as required.

When using *chortan* balls to make yogurt soups (*spas* or *madzoonabour*, see pp. 44 and 37), break two *chortan* balls with a sharp knife. The yogurt will have become powdery and should dissolve easily in water. Add the water— about 4 cups (1 l) to every two *chortan* balls—and stir well to dissolve. You can then use this liquid to prepare whichever type of yogurt soup you like (see next chapter).

surki

SPICED DRIED YOGURT

These are apple-sized balls of dried, spiced yogurt covered in thyme leaves, which are kept in airtight jars for months. They are excellent in salads such as *surki aghtsan* (p.100). They are also sometimes stored in olive oil. This keeps them soft and they are then used to make *zeytov surki* (p.105). *Surki*, the pride of Cilician Armenians, is known as *chaklish* by the Arabs of the region and as *chokeleg* by the local Assyrians and Turks.

Instead of yogurt, you can use cottage cheese, which is an excellent substitute for the *labna* made from milk.

The quantities given will make four fair-sized *surki* balls.

Labna made from 8 cups (2 l) yogurt (see p. 18) or 2 lb (1 kg) cottage cheese
2 teaspoons oregano
1 teaspoon ground cumin
1 teaspoon allspice
½ teaspoon chili powder
4 oz (100 g) fresh thyme leaves, coarsely chopped

1. Empty the *labna* into a bowl, knead it well, and mix in the oregano, cumin, allspice, and chili pepper. If you are using cottage cheese, mix and add the spices as with the *labna*, and blend in a blender or food processor to get the same smooth effect.
2. Divide the mixture into four and form balls.
3. Put on a tray and dry in the sun or, as with *chortan*, keep in a warm place until the *surki* balls are fairly dry.
4. Cover the *surki* balls completely with the thyme leaves and keep in a warm place for 24 hours.

soups

soups

First of all I must say that I find yogurt an excellent ingredient for
soup, perhaps because I was brought up on bowls of yogurt soup of one kind
or another. I am well aware that there are many other exciting soups—soups
made with vegetables, with meat, grains, fruit, even flowers, and of course clear
consommés, so popular in the European cuisine—but on a winter's night when
the wind is howling outside, and the rain is splashing against the window panes,
there is nothing better, I believe, than a bowl of hot yogurt soup to ease, warm,
and satisfy.

In the East, especially the Middle East, soups are often eaten as a meal
in themselves, accompanied by thick brown bread or thin flat *lavash*. Yogurt
soups play a unique role in the cuisine of the Middle East. They do not so far
exist in any other cuisine, surprisingly enough, not even in that of the Indian
subcontinent, which indeed possesses very few soups of any kind in its repertoire.
Naturally it is unheard of in the Far East, Africa—with the exception of Egypt,
Libya, and parts of Ethiopia—and the Americas.

Of all the Middle Eastern people I believe it is the Armenians and Iranians
who have used yogurt most, and yogurt soup particularly: the former seem to
prefer a simple treatment, in such favorites as *spas* and *madzoonabour*—a clear soup
of yogurt, chopped onions, and dried mint; the latter revel in rich, almost lavishly
ornamental, treatments as in *ash-e-jo*.

The possibilities for using yogurt in soups are limitless. It is an excellent
substitute for the sour cream popular throughout Eastern Europe and the
Balkans. It can often replace cream and mixes very well with most spices.
There is nothing better on a hot summer's day than a bowl of cold yogurt soup.
Certain vegetables and grains seem to have a great affinity with yogurt—spinach,
cucumber, onions, mint, rice, and barley, for example. Vegetables such as eggplant,
broccoli, and mushrooms have not been much used with yogurt but should
be. I hope the few dishes that I have included in this selection suggest that the
possibilities are rich. Indeed, anything goes with yogurt—well almost—so the best
way is to find out by experimenting.

suteresi chorba

WATERCRESS AND YOGURT SOUP

This is a Bulgarian soup also popular with Greeks and Turks. It is served chilled and is a delicious summer soup that also looks very attractive.

3 bunches watercress
4 cups (1 l) chicken stock
2 oz (50 g) walnuts
2½ cups (600 ml) yogurt
1 teaspoon salt
½ teaspoon ground white pepper

2 tablespoons lemon juice

GARNISH
some watercress sprigs
generous ½ cup (150 ml) yogurt

1. Wash the watercress; trim off the coarse stems and any yellow leaves.
2. Place the chicken stock in a saucepan, add the watercress, bring to a boil, and then simmer for about 15 minutes.
3. Strain the mixture into a colander, reserving the stock.
4. Place the watercress and walnuts in a blender and liquidize.
5. Pour this mixture into a large bowl, add the stock, and stir in the yogurt.
6. Season with the salt, pepper, and lemon juice, and leave to chill for a few hours in the refrigerator.
7. Taste and adjust seasoning if necessary.
8. Serve in individual bowls with a tablespoon of yogurt swirled into the center of each bowl of soup and garnished with a sprig of watercress.

ab dough khiar ba goosht-e-morgh

COLD YOGURT SOUP WITH CHICKEN

From Iran, this soup is substantial and different—a typical example of the cuisine of that land, making use of many ingredients. Although this is traditionally a soup, it could be served as a salad, as it is thick with chopped vegetables and meat.

2 medium-sized cucumbers
2½ cups (600 ml) yogurt
1 teaspoon dried tarragon
1 teaspoon thyme
2 leeks, washed and chopped
1 sprig fresh mint, chopped
1 tablespoon raisins
1 small onion, finely chopped

1 teaspoon salt
pinch of pepper
1 tablespoon walnuts, chopped
1 hard-boiled egg, thinly sliced
1 breast of chicken, boiled or grilled
2 tablespoons (1 oz/25 g) butter
1 tablespoon dried mint

1. Peel the cucumbers and chop them finely.
2. In a large bowl mix the yogurt and cucumber together.
3. Add the tarragon, thyme, leeks, mint, and raisins, and stir well.
4. Add the onion, salt, pepper, walnuts, and egg.
5. Bone the chicken, cut into fine pieces, and add to the soup. Mix well.
6. Melt the butter in a small saucepan, sauté the mint, and pour over the soup.
7. Serve cold.

tarator chorba

BULGARIAN YOGURT SOUP

Bulgaria is famed for its excellent yogurt and cheeses. This refreshing soup is ideal on a hot summer's day. Similar soups are found throughout the Balkans as well as Turkey.

2½ cups (600 ml) yogurt

1¼ cups (300 ml) milk

2 tablespoons sunflower or
   vegetable oil

1 tablespoon white vinegar

1 tablespoon lemon juice

4 oz (100 g) cooked meat,
   chopped finely

¼ cup cooked spaghetti,
   cut into short lengths

1 onion, finely chopped

2 tomatoes, blanched, peeled,
   and coarsely chopped

1 teaspoon salt

½ teaspoon white pepper

GARNISH

ice cubes

1 oz (25 g) walnuts, very finely
   chopped

1. Put the yogurt, milk, oil, vinegar, and lemon juice into a large bowl and whisk them together until smooth.
2. Stir in all the remaining ingredients and taste to adjust seasoning.
3. Spoon the soup into individual bowls, add an ice cube to each bowl, and then garnish with the chopped walnuts.

broccoli yogurt soup

A simple yet unusual soup. It can be served either hot or cold.

1 lb (½ kg) frozen broccoli
1 garlic clove
2½ cups (600 ml) chicken stock
½ teaspoon cayenne pepper
1 teaspoon salt
½ teaspoon black pepper

½ teaspoon dried basil
½ teaspoon ground cumin
1¼ cups (300 ml) yogurt
1 tablespoon flour if the soup
  is to be served hot

1. In a pan, cook the broccoli in a little boiling water for about 10 minutes, or until tender.
2. Discard water and allow the broccoli to cool.
3. Squeeze out excess water.
4. Spoon the broccoli into a blender and add the garlic, chicken stock, cayenne, salt, black pepper, basil, and ground cumin.
5. Blend until smooth.

FOR CHILLED SOUP
6. Add the yogurt to the blender and blend for 2 to 3 seconds.
7. Empty the contents of the blender into a glass bowl and chill in the refrigerator for 2 to 4 hours.

FOR HOT SOUP
6. Pour into a large saucepan and bring to a boil.
7. Stir 1 tablespoon of flour into the yogurt.
8. Lower the heat, add the yogurt, and stir well. Bring just to a boil and serve immediately.

cherkez chorbasi

CIRCASSIAN VEGETABLE SOUP WITH YOGURT

This is a Caucasian soup, popular with the Circassians, who are famed for their beautiful women and fierce dances. The soup itself is wholesome and tasty; some people may even call it beautiful too!

1 onion, peeled and sliced
1 carrot, peeled and sliced
4 oz (100 g) green beans, trimmed and sliced
4 oz (100 g) green peas
1 tablespoon long-grain rice, washed
1¼ cups (300 ml) tomato juice

2½ cups (600 ml) stock
½ teaspoon thyme
½ teaspoon paprika
1 teaspoon salt
½ teaspoon black pepper
2 bay leaves
generous ½ cup (150 ml) yogurt

1. Put all the ingredients except the yogurt into a large saucepan. If you are using frozen peas and beans rather than fresh ones, add them halfway through the cooking time.
2. Bring to a boil and then simmer until the vegetables are well cooked.
3. Stir in the yogurt, bring to just below boiling point, and serve immediately.

soups

soupa yaourti

YOGURT SOUP WITH TOMATO

This rather simple soup from Greece has a little wine added to the center of each bowl just before serving.

2½ cups (600 ml) yogurt
6 oz (175 g) rice, washed
4 tablespoons (50 g) butter
1 teaspoon salt
2 large fresh tomatoes, blanched
  and peeled

a little white wine
2 tablespoons finely chopped
  parsley

1. Drain the yogurt through a fine muslin cloth for about an hour to remove the whey.
2. Bring 6 cups (1½ l) water to a boil in a large saucepan, add the rice, butter, and salt, and bring back to a boil, stirring constantly.
3. Mash the tomatoes and add to the soup.
4. Lower the heat and simmer until the rice is tender.
5. Pour the yogurt into a mixing bowl and beat in 3 to 4 tablespoons of the soup until smooth.
6. Remove the soup from the heat and then stir in the yogurt mixture.
7. When well blended, ladle into individual bowls, spoon a little wine into each, and top with some chopped parsley.

armyansky borsht

ARMENIAN BORSHT

This soup, one of the most popular in Russia, is of Armenian origin. It makes use of yogurt instead of the Russian *smetana* (sour cream), which gives the soup a much simpler and lighter flavor. It is a rich soup, nevertheless. Serve it hot with *lavash* or *naan* bread.

1 medium beet

4 tablespoons (2 oz/50 g) butter

½ onion, finely chopped

1 medium carrot, scraped and chopped

1 stick celery, chopped

4 oz (100 g) cabbage, finely sliced

2 oz (50 g) mushrooms, finely sliced

1 small turnip, peeled and finely chopped

6–7 cups (1½–1¾ l) beef or lamb stock

1 lemon

2 teaspoons salt

1 teaspoon black pepper

1¼ cups (300 ml) yogurt

1. Place the whole beet, washed but unpeeled, in a small saucepan, cover with water, bring to a boil, and simmer until cooked—about 30 minutes.
2. Melt the butter in a large saucepan over moderate heat.
3. Add the prepared vegetables and sauté for a few minutes.
4. Add the stock and simmer until the vegetables are just tender.
5. Peel the beet, chop it, and add to the soup. Preparing the beets in this way should retain most of the red color.
6. Pierce holes in the lemon and drop it into the soup—this will give it extra tartness.
7. Add the seasoning and simmer for a further 10 to 15 minutes.
8. Taste and adjust seasoning if necessary.
9. Remove the lemon and discard it.
10. To serve, spoon the soup into individual bowls and place two tablespoons of yogurt in the center of each.

eshkeneh shirazi

FENUGREEK YOGURT SOUP

This classic Iranian soup is from the region of Shiraz, the heart of ancient Persia. Fenugreek, a popular spice known to the Romans as "Greek hay," is the seed of a plant belonging to the pea family. It is known as *chaiman* in Turkish and *shanbalileb* in Farsi. It has a bitter flavor and is used extensively in Iran, Armenia, and, particularly, the Gulf States. You can purchase it from Middle Eastern and Indian groceries. If you like the flavor of fenugreek, double the amount specified.

3 tablespoons (1½ oz/40 g) butter
1 onion, finely chopped
3 tablespoons flour
1 teaspoon fenugreek
2 oz (50 g) walnuts, coarsely chopped

1 teaspoon salt
½ teaspoon black pepper
2½ cups (600 ml) yogurt
2 tablespoons fresh parsley, chopped

1. In a large saucepan, melt the butter and fry the onion until golden brown.
2. Add the flour and stir until well blended.
3. Add the fenugreek and walnuts, and slowly stir in 5 cups (1¼ l) hot water.
4. Season with the salt and pepper.
5. Bring to a boil, then lower the heat and simmer for 20 minutes. By this time the soup will have thickened a little.
6. Empty the yogurt into a bowl, add a few tablespoons of the soup to it, and stir thoroughly.
7. Slowly pour the yogurt mixture into the soup pan, stirring constantly.
8. Heat through but do not allow to boil.
9. Serve immediately, garnished with freshly chopped parsley.

madzoonabour

YOGURT AND MINT SOUP

Armenian soups tend to be lighter and simpler than Iranian ones. This is by far the most popular of all Armenian soups and the most original in its simplicity. The centenarians of Kharapak in the Caucasus swear by this soup.

2½ cups (600 ml) yogurt
1 egg
1 teaspoon salt
¾ teaspoon black pepper
4 tablespoons (2 oz/50 g) butter
1 small onion, finely chopped

2 teaspoons mint, dried
  and crushed
2 thick slices bread, cut into
  ½ in (1 cm) cubes
cooking oil

1. Put the yogurt into a saucepan.
2. Break the egg into the yogurt and mix well with a wooden spoon.
3. Put on a low heat and stir continuously until the yogurt is just beginning to boil.
4. Add 2½ cups (600 ml) water, season with the salt and pepper, and return to the low heat.
5. Meanwhile, in a small saucepan, melt the butter, add the chopped onion and mint, and cook slowly until the onion is soft but not brown.
6. When ready pour into the soup.
7. Bring to a boil and simmer very gently for a few minutes.
8. Heat a little cooking oil in a small saucepan. When it is very hot add the cubes of bread and fry until golden brown. Remove from the oil and put into a bowl.
9. To serve, put the soup into individual bowls and add the croutons at the last moment—the quantity depending on taste and appetite.

istakoz çorbasi

LOBSTER SOUP

This recipe from Istanbul has French overtones—due probably to the many European hotels and restaurants in that cosmopolitan city.

2 tablespoons (1 oz/25 g) butter
2 onions, finely chopped
2 lb (1 kg) tomatoes, blanched,
   peeled, and sliced
1 garlic clove, crushed
1 teaspoon thyme—fresh if
   available
½ teaspoon ground fennel

¼ teaspoon ground nutmeg
1 teaspoon salt
½ teaspoon black pepper
generous ½ cup (150 ml)
   dry white wine
1 average-sized lobster, cooked
5 cups (1¼ l) fish stock
generous ½ cup (150 ml) yogurt

1. Melt the butter in a large saucepan and sauté the onions until they are soft and translucent.
2. Add the tomatoes, garlic, thyme, fennel, nutmeg, salt, and pepper; cover and simmer very gently for about ½ hour.
3. Add the wine, raise the heat, and boil for 3 to 4 minutes.
4. Cut the lobster flesh into small pieces and add half to the saucepan together with the fish stock.
5. Cook for a further 15 minutes; remove from the heat.
6. Either put the soup through a sieve or whisk it in a blender until it is smooth.
7. Return to the saucepan, add the remaining pieces of lobster flesh, and heat through.
8. Put the yogurt in a small bowl, add a few tablespoons of the soup, and beat with a wooden spoon until smooth.
9. Remove the soup from the heat, stir in the yogurt, and serve immediately.

havabour

CHICKEN WITH YOGURT SOUP

Armenian cuisine is rich in yogurt-based dishes. This is a typical recipe from that land. Compare this chicken soup with that from Iran (p. 26) to see the difference in approach and treatment. Serve with *lavash* or pita bread.

3 lb (1 kg) chicken, oven ready
  with giblets removed
1 carrot, washed, peeled, and
  thinly sliced
1 large onion, finely sliced
1 stalk celery, sliced into
  ½ in (1 cm) pieces

1¼ cups (300 ml) yogurt
2 eggs
1 teaspoon salt
½ teaspoon pepper
1 teaspoon ground fennel
1 teaspoon marjoram

1. Wash the chicken, put in a large saucepan or casserole, cover with 6 cups (1½ l) water, and bring to a boil. Remove the scum as it appears.
2. Add the carrot, onion, and celery, and simmer until the chicken is tender, about an hour.
3. Remove the chicken from the stock, leave to cool; then remove the flesh and cut it into thin strips.
4. Strain the stock, discard the vegetables, and return the stock to the pan.
5. Add the chicken.
6. In a bowl, combine the yogurt with the eggs and whisk.
7. Add a few tablespoons of the stock, season with salt and pepper, and stir well.
8. Add the yogurt mixture to the pan and, stirring constantly, heat through but do not allow to boil.
9. Serve hot, sprinkled with the fennel and marjoram.

punjabi lentil soup

Lentils, turmeric, and cumin give this soup a rich, earthy flavor. It is simple, nutritious, and easy to make. Use red lentils for extra color.

6 oz (175 g) lentils, cleaned and
  washed
2 tablespoons vegetable oil
1 onion, peeled and chopped
1–2 garlic cloves, finely chopped
1 teaspoon ground turmeric

½ teaspoon chili powder
1 teaspoon salt
½ teaspoon black pepper
1¼ cups (300 ml) yogurt
ground cumin to garnish

1. Soak the lentils for an hour in warm water.
2. In a saucepan heat the oil and sauté the onion and garlic until golden brown.
3. Drain the lentils and add the onion-garlic mixture.
4. Add the turmeric, chili powder, salt and pepper, and 5 cups (1¼ l) water. Bring to a boil, lower the heat, and simmer.
5. Cover the pan and cook for about an hour or until the lentils are cooked (red lentils will cook in less time, about 20 to 30 minutes).
6. Gently stir in the yogurt and leave long enough for the soup to heat through without boiling.
7. Serve immediately in soup bowls with a sprinkling of cumin.

duck soup

This soup comes from Russia, where, traditionally, sour cream is used rather than yogurt. I have found that yogurt is just as good as, if not better than, sour cream. The redcurrant jelly and red wine give the soup a very attractive appearance.

5 cups (1¼l) duck stock
  (chicken stock will do)
1 tablespoon redcurrant jelly
generous ½ cup (150 ml) dry
  red wine
2 tablespoons (1 oz/25 g) butter
2 shallots, chopped (or substitute
  finely chopped scallions)
1 teaspoon grated lemon rind

½ lb (250 g) duck meat, cooked
  and finely chopped
½ teaspoon salt
½ teaspoon pepper
generous ½ cup (150 ml) yogurt
1 egg
1 teaspoon finely chopped
  lemon verbena (optional)

1. In a large saucepan, bring the stock to a boil.
2. Stir in the redcurrant jelly and wine.
3. Stir well and boil for 5 to 8 minutes.
4. In a separate pan, melt the butter, add the shallots (or scallions), and sauté for 2 minutes.
5. Add the lemon rind and meat and cook for 5 more minutes.
6. Stir this mixture into the pan of stock, add the salt and pepper, and stir thoroughly.
7. Put the yogurt into a small bowl with the egg and beat thoroughly.
8. Add a tablespoon of the hot stock to the yogurt and then add the mixture to the soup.
9. Stir constantly until the soup has thickened, but do not boil.
10. Before serving, garnish with lemon verbena.
11. Serve immediately.

soup-e-aroosi

WEDDING SOUP

This is a Turcoman dish, popular in Turkey and Iranian Azerbaijan. It is, as the name suggests, the soup of any village wedding. Simple and tasty.

4 tablespoons (2 oz/50 g) butter
1 onion, thinly sliced
1 lb (½ kg) lean lamb, cut into 1 in
  (3 cm) pieces (beef can be
  substituted for the lamb)

2–3 teaspoons salt
½ teaspoon black pepper
2 eggs
1 tablespoon lemon juice
2 tablespoons yogurt

1. In a large saucepan, melt the butter and sauté the onion until golden brown.
2. Add the meat and sauté for 5 to 8 minutes or until nicely browned.
3. Add 7¼ cups (1¾ l) water and simmer for ½ hour or until meat is tender, removing any scum that may appear on the surface.
4. Add the salt and pepper and mix well.
5. In a small bowl, beat together the eggs, lemon juice, and yogurt.
6. Stir 3 tablespoons of the stock into the yogurt mixture and then 3 more.
7. Pour the yogurt mixture into the soup. Taste and adjust seasoning, if necessary.
8. Serve immediately.

spas

BARLEY SOUP WITH DRIED YOGURT

A classic of the Armenian cuisine. It is traditionally prepared with *chortan* (p. 20); however plain yogurt will do just as well.

3 oz (75 g) pearl barley

2 cups (450 ml) plain yogurt
  or 2 *chortan* balls

4 eggs

1 tablespoon (15 g) flour

1 small onion, finely chopped

2 tablespoons (1 oz/25 g) butter

2 teaspoons salt

1 level teaspoon ground black
  pepper

2 teaspoons finely chopped mint

2 teaspoons finely chopped parsley
  or cilantro

1. Soak barley in cold water overnight.
2. Drain barley and put in a large saucepan with about 5 cups (1¼ l) water and cook for ½ hour or until tender.
3. Drain through a fine sieve.
4. Put yogurt into a large bowl, add 5 cups (1¼ l) water, and mix until well blended. If you are using *chortan* balls, break them with a knife and mix with 7¼ cups (1¾ l) water.
5. Break the eggs into a saucepan and whisk in the flour, a little at time.
6. Stir in the yogurt (or *chortan*) mixture and place over moderate heat.
7. Whisk constantly in one direction to prevent curdling, bring almost to boiling point, and then lower the heat quickly.
8. Allow to simmer very gently for 2 to 3 minutes until the mixture thickens slightly.
9. Meanwhile, melt the butter in a small pan and fry the onion until soft and just beginning to brown.
10. Stir the barley, cooked onion, salt, and black pepper into the soup and simmer for another minute.
11. When ready to serve, sprinkle with the finely chopped fresh herbs.

printzov tanabour

Follow the recipe on p. 44 but use rice instead of barley. There is no need to soak the rice, simply wash it thoroughly and then cook until tender and drain. This soup has a reputation for being beneficial to the sick and those with stomach troubles.

chicken and barley soup with yogurt

Follow the recipe for *spas* (p. 44) but use 7¼ cups (1¾ l) chicken stock instead of water.

ash-e-jo

BARLEY SOUP

A thick wholesome soup of barley, vegetables, and yogurt from northern Iran, beloved by the Kurds and Turks of the region. Serve with bread.

2 oz (50 g) dried red kidney beans	1 onion, finely chopped
2 oz (50 g) dried chickpeas	3 oz (75 g) barley
4 oz (100 g) whole brown lentils	3 oz (75 g) spinach, chopped
2 teaspoons salt	1½ oz (40 g) parsley, chopped
black pepper to taste	4 oz (100 g) leeks, chopped
½ teaspoon turmeric	½ cup chopped fresh dill or cilantro
2 tablespoons (1 oz/25 g) butter	1¼ cups (300 ml) yogurt

1. Soak the kidney beans and chickpeas in water overnight.
2. In a large saucepan, combine the chickpeas, kidney beans, lentils, 5 cups (1¼ l) water, and the salt, pepper, and turmeric.

3. Meanwhile, melt the butter in a small pan and sauté the onion until it is soft and brown.
4. Add the onion and barley to the saucepan.
5. Bring to a boil and allow to simmer for 45 minutes to 1 hour.
6. Add the chopped vegetables and herbs, and continue simmering for another 20 to 30 minutes or until the beans, barley, and chickpeas are tender. Add a little more water if necessary.
7. Remove the soup from the heat and slowly stir in the yogurt.
8. Serve immediately.

tutmaj

Another classic Armenian yogurt soup. Traditionally made with *chortan* (see p. 20) but plain yogurt can be used instead. This version uses homemade noodles but any form of traditional small pasta is suitable. Small balls of ground meat can be added to give more substance to the dish, which, with bread, is often eaten as a main meal.

4 cups (1 l) yogurt

2 egg yolks

4–5 oz (125–150 g) noodles

½ lb (250 g) ground meat, seasoned and shaped into small marble-sized rissoles and fried (optional)

1 teaspoon salt

½ teaspoon pepper

1 onion, finely chopped

4 tablespoons (2 oz/50 g) butter

2 tablespoons dried mint, crushed

1. In a large pan, bring the yogurt and the egg yolks slowly to a boil, beating constantly.
2. Pour in 2 cups (½ l) water and add the noodles—also the fried meatballs if you are including them.
3. Add the salt and pepper, bring to a boil, lower the heat, and simmer for 8 to 10 minutes until the pasta is just cooked.
4. Meanwhile, fry the onions in the butter.
5. Add the mint to the onions, stir, fry a little longer, and then remove from the heat.
6. Pour the onion mixture into the soup. Stir well.
7. Serve immediately.

ash-e-mast

IRANIAN YOGURT SOUP

This soup, like most Iranian dishes, is rich and elaborate—more like a stew.
It is very filling and, as an added bonus, it uses inexpensive ingredients. It is
particularly popular with the Azerbaijani Turks.

1 oz (25 g) dried chickpeas
1 oz (25 g) dried navy beans
2 oz (50 g) whole brown lentils
6 oz (175 g) stewing lamb or
   lamb shank
½ teaspoon turmeric

2 tablespoons (1 oz/25 g) butter
1 onion, finely chopped
1 teaspoon salt
2 oz (50 g) rice, washed
2 cups (½ l) yogurt

1. Soak the chickpeas, navy beans, and lentils in cold water overnight.
2. Melt the butter and sauté the onion until it is soft and golden brown.
3. Add the meat and cook for 5 to 10 minutes, stirring occasionally.
4. Drain and rinse the chickpeas, beans, and lentils, and add to the saucepan,
   together with the turmeric, salt, and rice, and 8 cups (2 l) water.
5. Cover and simmer for 1½ hours or until cooked, adding more water if
   necessary.
6. When all the ingredients are cooked, remove the pan from the heat.
7. Remove the meat from the soup and reduce to a pulp either with a blender or a
   mortar and pestle.
8. Return the meat pulp to the soup, stir, and adjust seasoning, if necessary.
9. Beat the yogurt in a small bowl and stir some of the soup into it.
10. Slowly pour the yogurt into the soup, heat through without boiling,
    and serve immediately.

halim bademjan

EGGPLANT SOUP

This thick soup from Iran is really a meal in itself, ideal on a cold winter's night. You can substitute two chicken breasts for the lamb if you like.

1 large eggplant
6 tablespoons (3 oz/75 g) butter
2 medium onions, very finely
  chopped
1 lb (½ kg) lamb, cut into 1½–2 in
  (4–5 cm) pieces
1 oz (25 g) dried chickpeas, soaked
  in cold water overnight

1½ oz (40 g) whole brown lentils,
  washed
3 oz (75 g) long-grain rice, washed
1 teaspoon turmeric
2 teaspoons salt
¼ teaspoon black pepper
1¼ cups (300 ml) yogurt
¼ teaspoon cinnamon

1. Cut the top off the eggplant, peel the eggplant, and slice thinly.
2. If preferred, sprinkle the slices with salt, and set aside for 30 minutes, then rinse under cold water and pat dry with paper towel.
3. Melt 2 tablespoons (1 oz/25 g) butter in a large saucepan and cook the onions until golden brown.
4. Add the meat, chickpeas, lentils, rice, 2½ cups (600 ml) water, turmeric, salt, and pepper.
5. Bring to a boil, cover, and simmer for about an hour.
6. Melt the remaining 4 tablespoons (2 oz/50 g) butter in a frying pan and sauté the eggplant slices until they are brown on both sides. Add more butter if necessary.
7. Add the eggplants to the soup, cover, and simmer for a further 30 to 40 minutes, until everything, especially the chickpeas, is tender.
8. Using a slotted spoon, transfer the meat and eggplant pieces to a blender.
9. Blend with just sufficient stock to form a thick paste.
10. Return the paste to the soup and stir well.
11. Remove the soup from the heat.
12. Stir in the yogurt, sprinkle with cinnamon, and serve immediately.

madzoonov kufte

WHEAT AND MEATBALLS IN YOGURT SAUCE

A regional specialty from the city of Gaziantep in southern Turkey. It is also popular with Syrians, who call it *kibbeh-bi-laban*. This is more than a soup. It becomes a hearty meal when served with pickles and bread. Instead of the chicken you can use 3 lb (1½ kg) lamb or beef cut into 2 in (5 cm) cubes.

SERVES SIX TO EIGHT

½ lb (250 g) fresh lamb's suet from around the kidneys or 2 sticks (½ lb/250 g) butter

3 lb (1½ kg) chicken, cut into joints

4 oz (100 g) dried chickpeas, soaked overnight

3 teaspoons salt

5–6 cups (1¼–1½ l) yogurt

2 eggs

4 tablespoons (2 oz/50 g) butter

1 tablespoon dried mint

KUFTE

9 oz (275 g) fine bulgar

12 oz (350 g) lean lamb, finely ground

1 onion, finely chopped

2 teaspoons salt

1 teaspoon chili powder

1. Divide the fat into small pieces about the size of a pea, roll each one between the palms to form small balls, and refrigerate.
2. Half-fill a large saucepan with water, add the chicken joints and chickpeas, and bring to a boil.
3. Remove any scum that gathers on the surface.
4. Cook until the meat and chickpeas are tender, at least 1 hour. Season with the salt.
5. Meanwhile, prepare the *kufte*. Wash the bulgar, pour away excess water, and spread the bulgar on a baking sheet for about 10 minutes.
6. Add the ground meat, onion, salt, chili powder, and 2 tablespoons of cold water, and mix well.
7. Knead the mixture by placing both your hands on it and taking hold of two handfuls, squeezing, pressing down, and pushing it away from you. Repeat this several times.

8. Gather the mixture up into a ball in the middle of the baking sheet and knead again in the same way. Repeat several times.

9. Knead the mixture until it is well blended and smooth. It should take about 10 to 15 minutes. You will find it much easier if you sprinkle some water over it occasionally and keep your hands damp.

10. Break off small pieces of the *kufte* about the size of a walnut and roll between the palms to make balls.

11. Make a hole inside each with your forefinger. The simplest way to do this is to hold the ball of *kufte* in one hand, push the forefinger of the other hand inside the ball and press all around the wall, turning the ball while pressing.

12. Put a ball of suet or butter into the hole.

13. Bring the edges of the opening together and seal.

14. Now roll the ball between your palms to give it a round shape and smooth outer surface.

15. Repeat this with all the *kufte*, occasionally dipping your hands into water to avoid them sticking.

16. When all the suet or butter has been used, simply make small marble-sized *kufte* balls without filling.

17. Mix the yogurt and eggs together in a small bowl.

18. Add a little of the hot chicken stock to the yogurt and stir it in.

19. Add the yogurt sauce to the large pan of stock with the chicken and chickpeas.

20. Simmer very gently.

21. In a small saucepan, melt the butter, add the mint, stirring for 1 to 2 minutes, and pour into the yogurt soup.

22. Add the *kufte* balls to the soup and simmer, very gently, for 10 to 15 minutes until the *kufte* is cooked.

23. Serve hot, placing several *kufte* in each bowl with some of the chickpeas and chicken and plenty of the liquid.

dovga

YOGURT SOUP WITH MEATBALLS

A popular soup in Azerbaijan, Russia, and northern Iran. *Dovga* is rich in flavor and is served hot with *lavash*, pita, or *naan* bread.

½ lb (250 g) ground beef or lamb
1 onion, finely chopped
salt and black pepper to taste
4 cups (1 l) yogurt
1 tablespoon (15 g) flour
5 cups (1¼ l) stock or water
1 oz (25 g) basmati rice, washed
4½ oz (110 g) chopped spinach
2 oz (50 g) dried chickpeas, soaked

overnight, cooked in water until
just tender, and drained; or use
drained, canned chickpeas
3 tablespoons finely chopped
parsley
2 scallions, finely chopped
3 tablespoons fresh dill, chopped
(or 1 tablespoon dried dill)

1. In a large bowl mix the meat, onion, salt, and pepper.
2. Knead until well mixed and smooth.
3. Make small walnut-sized balls and put on one side.
4. Pour the yogurt into a large saucepan and add the flour, mixed with a little stock or water. Add the rest of the stock or water and beat until well blended.
5. Season with a little salt and pepper.
6. Add the meatballs and rice; simmer on a low heat for 12 to 15 minutes, stirring gently and very frequently.
7. Add the spinach and the cooked chickpeas and simmer for a further 10 to 12 minutes until the rice is cooked and the meat is tender.
8. Add the parsley, onion, scallions, and dill, and cook for a further 5 minutes.
9. Serve immediately.

mantabour

DUMPLINGS IN A YOGURT SOUP

This is a fascinating soup from Anatolia which, in fact, originated in China and Korea. *Manta* is a Chinese dumpling similar to ravioli, and was probably brought to the Middle East by the Mongolian tribes in their search for pastures.

SERVES SIX

DOUGH
12 oz (350 g) all-purpose flour
1 egg
2 tablespoons (1 oz/25 g) butter,
   melted
½ teaspoon salt

FILLING
¾ lb (350 g) ground lamb or beef
1 large onion, finely chopped
2 tablespoons finely chopped
   parsley

1 teaspoon salt
½ teaspoon black pepper

SOUP
7–9 cups (1¾–2¼ l) stock
salt and pepper to taste
4 tablespoons (2 oz/50 g) butter
1 large onion, finely chopped
1 tablespoon dried mint
4 cups (1 l) yogurt
2 eggs

1. Place the flour in a large mixing bowl and make a hollow in the middle.
2. Add the egg, butter, 1 cup (200 ml) water, and salt, and knead for 10 to 15 minutes until the dough is soft and elastic.
3. Shape the dough into a ball, cover with a dish towel, and leave to rest for 30 to 40 minutes.
4. Place all the filling ingredients in another bowl and knead well with damp hands.
5. For ease in handling divide the dough into two or three parts.
6. Flour a work surface and roll out one part of the dough until paper thin.
7. Cut the pastry into 2 in (5 cm) squares.
8. Repeat with the remaining dough.

9. Place a small, cherry-sized ball of the meat mixture on a square.
10. Dip a finger in cold water and moisten the edges of the square.
11. Fold the pastry over to form a triangle and pinch the edges together to seal.
12. Keeping your fingers moist, bring the two folded corners together and pinch firmly.
13. Repeat with the remaining squares of dough. If there is any meat mixture left over, form into small balls and cook with the dumplings.
14. The alternative way of shaping the dumplings is to cut the pastry into 2 in (5 cm) circles, place a little of the meat mixture in the center, and then bring the pastry up around the meat; collect the edges together and pinch to seal—thus forming small bags.
15. Bring the stock to a boil in a large saucepan and season with salt and pepper to taste.
16. Add the dumplings and simmer for 15 to 20 minutes until tender.
17. In a small saucepan, melt the butter and sauté the onion until golden brown.
18. Stir in the mint and remove from the heat.
19. Pour the yogurt into a large bowl and beat in the eggs.
20. Spoon about 2½ cups (600 ml) of the boiling stock into the yogurt and stir well.
21. Slowly pour the yogurt mixture into the large saucepan, stir, and cook for 5 to 10 minutes, but do not let it boil.
22. Add the onion mixture, cook for a further 2 to 3 minutes, and then serve immediately.

appetizers

apple and celery cream

A simple and delightful hors d'oeuvre with celery giving it bite.

3 red apples
3 sticks of celery
1 tablespoon chopped chervil
1 teaspoon finely chopped parsley

generous ½ cup (150 ml) yogurt
⅓ cup (75 ml) heavy cream
1 teaspoon allspice to garnish

1. Core the apples.
2. Either mince the apples and celery or chop very finely.
3. Place in a bowl and stir in the chervil and parsley.
4. Beat the yogurt and cream together, pour over the salad, and mix.
5. Serve the salad in individual dishes, sprinkled with a little allspice.

artichokes with yogurt

Though normally a bland vegetable, artichoke acquires a very good flavor when combined with yogurt and spices.

juice of 1 lemon (retain the skin)
4 small artichokes
generous ½ cup (150 ml) olive oil
1 teaspoon coriander seeds

1 teaspoon dried marjoram
1 teaspoon dried basil
salt and pepper to taste
1¼ cups (300 ml) yogurt

1. Half-fill a large saucepan with water, add 2 teaspoons lemon juice, and bring to a boil. Leave simmering gently while you prepare the artichokes.

2. Cut the stalks from the artichokes and remove any coarse outer leaves.
3. Slice off the top third of each artichoke and discard.
4. Rub the inside of the lemon skin over the cut edges.
5. With kitchen scissors, snip ¼ in (½ cm) off the top of the remaining leaves and rub the cut edges again with the lemon skin.
6. Drop the artichokes into the simmering water and parboil for about 10 minutes.
7. Drain them, plunge into cold water, and drain again.
8. Put 2½ cups (600 ml) water into a saucepan with the oil, lemon juice, coriander seeds, marjoram, basil, and salt and pepper, and bring to a boil.
9. Add the artichokes and cook, uncovered, for a further 20 to 30 minutes. They are cooked when the bases can be pierced easily with a sharp knife.
10. Drain the artichokes but retain the juices. When cool enough to handle, spread out the top leaves and pull out the prickly leaves surrounding the hairy choke.
11. With a teaspoon scrape out the choke and discard, then press the leaves back together again.
12. Place in the refrigerator to chill.
13. Before serving, beat the yogurt and stir in the reserved juices.
14. When ready to serve, place the artichokes in small bowls and spoon the yogurt sauce over the top of each.

dabgevadz sumpoog

FRIED EGGPLANT WITH YOGURT

A traditional recipe from Cilician Armenia, this is popular in Turkey and Syria. Apart from being a tasty appetizer, it also makes a good side dish for lamb kebab.

2 large eggplants
salt
olive or vegetable oil

1¼ cups (300 ml) garlic yogurt sauce (see p. 247)
1 teaspoon dried mint

1. Slice the heads and tails from the eggplants.
2. Cut the eggplants crosswise into ½ in (1 cm) slices.
3. If preferred, arrange slices on a large plate, sprinkle with salt, and leave for ½ hour, then rinse under cold water and dry on paper towels.
4. Pour some oil into a large saucepan or frying pan and heat.
5. Fry some of the eggplant slices on both sides until a light golden brown. Remove to absorbent paper towel.
6. Repeat with the remaining slices.
7. Arrange half the slices over a large plate.
8. Pour some of the yogurt sauce over them and arrange the remaining slices on top.
9. Pour the rest of the yogurt over the top and sprinkle with the mint.

kabak tavasi

FRIED ZUCCHINI WITH YOGURT

A Turkish-Armenian variation.

4 zucchinis, ends removed, sliced crosswise into ½ in (1 cm) pieces
olive or vegetable oil

1¼ cups (300 ml) garlic yogurt sauce (see p. 247)
1 teaspoon mint

Prepare in the same way as fried eggplant (above).

madznov sumpoogi aghtsan

EGGPLANT PURÉE WITH YOGURT

A traditional Armenian recipe. It is ideal as an appetizer to be eaten with warm pita or *lavash*. You can vary the number of chilies according to taste.

3 large eggplants	1¼ cups (300 ml) yogurt
¼ cup (60 ml) olive oil	6 green chilis
1 tablespoon lemon juice	3 garlic cloves
salt to taste	1 tablespoon finely chopped parsley

1. Pierce each eggplant a few times with a sharp knife.
2. Either place them on one of the shelves in the center of a hot oven or place on skewers and grill over a charcoal fire.
3. Cook until they are soft when poked with a finger.
4. Allow to cool; cut off stems and peel off the skin.
5. Cut the flesh into pieces.
6. Heat the olive oil in a frying pan, add the eggplant flesh, and fry for a few minutes.
7. Place the flesh in a large bowl, add the lemon juice, salt, and yogurt, and mash with a fork until smooth. Leave to cool.
8. Cook the green chilis under the broiler, turning until cooked on all sides.
9. Cut the stalk ends off and remove the skins from three.
10. Using a mortar and pestle, crush 3 of the chilis and garlic with ½ teaspoon of salt until smooth.
11. Stir into the eggplant mixture.
12. Spread the purée over a large plate.
13. Coarsely chop the remaining chilis and use to garnish the salad, together with the chopped parsley.

avocado salad

A refreshing and attractive appetizer. You could also add pieces of feta cheese.

2 ripe avocados
salt
½ grapefruit, separated
   into segments
1 tangerine, separated

into segments
1 slice melon, cut into cubes
8 stuffed olives
generous ½ cup (150 ml) Orga's
   yogurt dressing (see p. 245)

1. Cut the avocados in half lengthwise and remove the pits.
2. Scoop out the flesh, cut into cubes, and place in a large bowl. Reserve the shells.
3. Sprinkle the avocado flesh with a little salt.
4. Remove the skin from the grapefruit and tangerine segments and cut the flesh into pieces.
5. Add these to the bowl, together with the melon pieces and the stuffed olives.
6. Toss all the fruits together and refrigerate for a few hours.
7. Prepare the yogurt dressing.
8. Just before serving, spoon the fruits into the avocado shells and pour a little of the dressing over each.

bakla

This is an adaptation of a Turkish–Kurdish dish. You can omit the scallions and substitute finely sliced Spanish onions. Try garnishing it with sliced tomatoes and cucumber. Serve with pita bread. It is a good accompaniment to all roast and cooked meat and fowl dishes.

1 lb (½ kg) fresh fava beans
  (If you have young beans then do
  not shell them but use them as
  they are. Otherwise use 1 lb [½ kg]
  shelled beans.)
2 teaspoons salt
1 tablespoon lemon juice
2 teaspoons chopped dill or
  1 teaspoon dried dill
1 teaspoon chopped mint

1 teaspoon oregano
½ teaspoon black pepper
generous ½ cup (150 ml) olive oil
4 scallions or 1 Spanish onion,
  finely sliced
1¼ cups (300 ml) garlic yogurt sauce
  (see p. 247)
1 teaspoon ground cumin
½ teaspoon cayenne pepper

1. If using young beans, cut off the tops of the pods and string the sides. Wash thoroughly and cut into 1 in (3 cm) lengths. Otherwise simply wash the beans.
2. Into a large saucepan put the beans, salt, lemon juice, dill, mint, oregano, and black pepper.
3. Meanwhile, heat the oil in a small pan and fry the onions until soft.
4. Add the onions and the oil to the large saucepan together with 1¼ cups (300 ml) water.
5. Cook for about an hour or until the beans are tender and the water has reduced substantially.
6. Chill in the refrigerator for a few hours.
7. Whisk the garlic yogurt sauce and pour over the beans.
8. Sprinkle with cumin and cayenne pepper.
9. Serve cold as an appetizer.

kashk-e kadoo

ZUCCHINI WITH YOGURT

This Iranian appetizer is traditionally made with liquid whey, but I find that
it works better with yogurt. As well as being an appetizer, this makes a tasty
vegetable dish to serve with lamb or poultry.

3 medium-to-large zucchinis
3 tablespoons (1½ oz/40 g) butter
1 onion, finely chopped
1 garlic clove, crushed
½ teaspoon turmeric

1 teaspoon salt
2 cups (450 ml) yogurt, stabilized
   with 1 tablespoon flour (see p. 17)
1 teaspoon dried mint

1. Remove heads and tails from the zucchinis then cut each zucchini
   into four, lengthwise.
2. Cut each quarter into ¼ in (½ cm) pieces.
3. Melt 2 tablespoons (1 oz/25 g) butter in a saucepan, add the onion and garlic,
   and sauté until the onion is golden brown.
4. Add the zucchinis and sauté, stirring occasionally for a few minutes.
5. Stir in the turmeric, salt, and ⅓ cup (75 ml) water and simmer, stirring
   occasionally, until the liquid has been absorbed and the zucchinis are just
   tender.
6. Very slowly stir in the yogurt and heat through, but do not boil.
7. Melt the remaining 1 tablespoon (½ oz/15 g) butter in a small pan, add the
   mint, and cook for 2 to 3 minutes.
8. Spoon the zucchinis and yogurt into a serving dish and then pour the butter
   and mint mixture over the top.
9. Serve immediately.

tzajiki

CUCUMBER AND YOGURT DIP

This Greek dip is similar to the Armenian *jajig* (see p. 92), with a few additional ingredients. Spread it over bread or crackers, or serve it with hot pita bread.

½ cucumber, peeled
1 cup (200 ml) yogurt
1 garlic clove, finely chopped
2 tablespoons olive oil
1 teaspoon vinegar

1 tablespoon heavy cream
½ teaspoon confectioner's sugar
salt and pepper to taste
1 tablespoon finely chopped mint
  or 1 teaspoon dried mint

1. Chop the cucumber very finely.
2. Place in a sieve and leave for ½ hour to drain.
3. In a bowl, mix all the other ingredients, except the mint.
4. Dry the cucumber on a paper towel, then add to the yogurt mixture and mix thoroughly.
5. Transfer to a salad bowl and sprinkle with mint.
6. Chill in the refrigerator for ½ to 1 hour.
7. Serve as a dip.

kaleh joosh

DATES AND WALNUTS WITH YOGURT

This is an Iranian dish, also popular in Iraq. It is traditionally made with liquid whey (*kashk*) but yogurt is an excellent substitute.

3 tablespoons (1½ oz/40 g) butter
1 onion, finely chopped
1 teaspoon dried mint
1 garlic clove, crushed
2½ cups (600 ml) yogurt, stabilized with 1 egg (see p. 17)

½ teaspoon saffron dissolved in 1 tablespoon boiling water
½ lb (250 g) pitted dates, thinly sliced lengthwise
2 oz (50 g) walnuts, roughly chopped

1. Melt the butter in a saucepan and sauté the onion, mint, and garlic until the onion is soft.
2. Stir in the stabilized yogurt, bring just to a boil, and remove immediately from the heat.
3. Stir in the saffron, dates, and walnuts.
4. Spoon into a serving dish.
5. Serve warm with bread.

fruit cup

A tangy appetizer that makes an excellent use of fruit and yogurt.

1 large grapefruit

2 oranges

1 can pineapple chunks or 1 small
   fresh pineapple, peeled and cut
   into small cubes

1¼ cups (300 ml) yogurt

2 tablespoons sugar or
   2 tablespoons honey

fresh mint leaves, to garnish

1. Peel the grapefruit and oranges and divide the fruit into segments.
2. Remove the skin from the segments and then cut the fruit into small pieces.
3. Mix all the fruit in a large bowl and chill in the refrigerator for a few hours.
4. At the same time mix the yogurt and sugar or honey together, and chill.
5. Spoon the fruit into a large glass bowl or into individual glasses and spoon the yogurt over the fruit.
6. Garnish with fresh mint leaves and serve chilled.

zakuska

MUSHROOMS ON TOAST

This popular and traditional Russian dish is normally served with sour cream but yogurt is an excellent substitute. As well as being a tasty appetizer, this makes a quickly prepared snack.

4 tablespoons (2 oz/50 g) butter
4 scallions, chopped
2 teaspoons paprika
1 lb (½ kg) mushrooms, wiped clean and sliced thickly
1 tablespoon lemon juice
2 tablespoons flour

2 cups (450 ml) yogurt
1 teaspoon salt
½ teaspoon black pepper
4 large slices whole wheat or rye bread
a little chopped fresh dill or parsley

1. Melt the butter in a saucepan and sauté the onions until soft.
2. Stir in the paprika and cook for 1 minute.
3. Add the mushrooms and lemon juice to the pan and sauté for about 5 minutes, stirring occasionally.
4. Add the flour and stir in well.
5. Add the yogurt slowly, stirring constantly until the mixture thickens.
6. Season with the salt and pepper.
7. Meanwhile, remove the crusts and then toast the slices of bread.
8. Cut each slice into four triangles and either arrange over a large serving plate or on individual plates.
9. Spoon the mushroom mixture over the toast and garnish with the fresh dill or parsley.

salad e nokhod ba mast

YOGURT AND GREEN PEA SALAD

A delightful appetizer from Iran, where it is an integral part of any self-respecting buffet table. Scoop it up with bread or lettuce leaves.

1 lb (½ kg) potatoes, preferably new

4 oz (125 g) green peas, fresh or frozen

about ½ cup (125 g) *labna* made from 2½ cups (600 ml) yogurt (see p. 18)

3 tablespoons chopped fresh dill or

2 tablespoons dried dill

¼ cup (60 ml) olive oil

2 tablespoons lemon juice

2 dill pickles, thinly sliced

salt and pepper to taste

lettuce leaves

a few washed radishes, to garnish

1. Boil the potatoes until tender, cool, peel, and cut into ½ in (1 cm) cubes.
2. Cook the peas until tender.
3. Put the potatoes into a large salad bowl with the peas.
4. Mix in the *labna*, dill, olive oil, lemon juice, dill pickles, and salt and pepper to taste.
5. Leave in the refrigerator to chill for a few hours.
6. Serve on lettuce leaves, garnished with a few radishes.

pear cocktail

An attractive starter or a cocktail dish that goes over well at parties.

2 large ripe pears
generous ½ cup (150 ml) yogurt
¼ teaspoon salt
a pinch of black pepper
a few drops Worcestershire sauce

2 tablespoons grated cheese
 (e.g. Cheddar, feta, Edam)
2 tablespoons chopped mixed nuts
a little paprika

1. Peel, halve, and core the pears.
2. In a small bowl mix together the yogurt, salt, pepper,
   Worcestershire sauce, cheese, and nuts.
3. Spoon this mixture into the cavity of each pear half.
4. Chill and serve sprinkled with a little paprika.

madznov dakdegh

GREEN PEPPERS WITH YOGURT

Another Armenian appetizer; it is served cold spread on pita or any other bread.

4 large green peppers
1¼ cups (300 ml) garlic yogurt sauce
 (see p. 247)

½ teaspoon cumin
½ teaspoon black pepper
3 tomatoes, quartered (optional)

1. Wash the green peppers and cut out the stems and seeds.
2. Cook under the broiler or over a charcoal fire, turning occasionally until they
   are well cooked all over.
3. Remove from the heat and leave to cool.
4. Peel off the outer skins.
5. Quarter each pepper and then cut into very thin slices.
6. Arrange the slices in a serving dish and stir in the yogurt sauce.
7. Sprinkle with the cumin and black pepper and decorate with the tomatoes.

shomin

SPINACH AND YOGURT SALAD

This is a classic of the Armenian cuisine. It is superb to look at with its dazzling combination of colors, and what is more, it is simple to make. Serve it as an appetizer or as an accompaniment to roast and grilled meats.

1 lb (½ kg) fresh or frozen spinach
4 tablespoons (2 oz/50 g) butter
1 small onion, finely chopped
salt and black pepper to taste
1¼ cups (300 ml) yogurt

2 garlic cloves, crushed
paprika
2 tablespoons finely chopped
   toasted walnuts (optional)

1. Strip the leaves from the stalks of the fresh spinach and wash very thoroughly to remove all the grit and sand. (Thaw out frozen spinach.)
2. Half-fill a large pan with water, bring to a boil, and add the spinach.
3. Simmer for about 10 minutes or until the spinach is just cooked.
4. Strain into a colander and leave until cool enough to handle.
5. Using your hands, squeeze out as much of the water as possible.
6. Chop the spinach.
7. Melt the butter in a large frying pan and fry the onion until it is soft and just beginning to brown.
8. Add the chopped spinach and fry for a further 5 minutes.
9. Season to taste with the salt and black pepper.
10. Keep on a low heat while you mix the yogurt and crushed garlic together in a small bowl.
11. Divide the spinach into four portions and arrange each on a small plate in a circular shape.
12. Spoon some of the yogurt into the center of each circle and then sprinkle the yogurt with just a little paprika.
13. If you like, sprinkle a few chopped walnuts over the top.

znonit beshamenet

RADISHES WITH YOGURT

This Israeli salad is normally made with sour cream—it has Eastern European origins. I have substituted plain yogurt and have found that it is a great improvement.

3 teaspoons wine vinegar
1 teaspoon white sugar
1 teaspoon salt
½ teaspoon black pepper

1¼ cups (300 ml) yogurt
20 or so radishes
1 small onion

1. Mix the vinegar, sugar, salt, pepper, and yogurt in a small bowl and leave in the refrigerator to chill.
2. Trim and wash the radishes.
3. Cut the radishes crosswise into thin slices.
4. Peel the onion and cut crosswise into thin slices.
5. Push the onion slices out into rings.
6. Put the radishes and onion into a large salad bowl.
7. Pour the dressing over the top and mix well.
8. Refrigerate for an hour or so and serve well chilled.

tzoo-yev-madzoon

EGGS WITH YOGURT AND HERB DRESSING

From Caucasian Armenia, this is a decorative dish of hard-boiled eggs on a bed
of lettuce leaves with chopped vegetables and a delicious fresh-tasting dressing.
It can be served either as an hors d'oeuvre or as the main dish for a summer lunch.

1 round lettuce, coarse outer leaves
  discarded, separated into leaves,
  and washed
8 hard-boiled eggs, shelled
8 black olives, halved and stoned
2 bunches watercress, washed and
  shaken dry
10 large radishes, thinly sliced
1 large green pepper, seeded and
  thinly sliced
3 medium carrots, scraped
  and grated

DRESSING
1¼ cups (300 ml) yogurt
2 teaspoons lemon juice
1 teaspoon tarragon vinegar
2 tablespoons chopped fresh chives
1 teaspoon dried dill
1 tablespoon chopped parsley
1 teaspoon paprika
½ teaspoon salt
¼ teaspoon black pepper

1. Arrange the lettuce leaves on a large serving platter.
2. Slice the eggs in half lengthwise and then place them around the edge
   of the platter, cut-side down.
3. Top each egg half with half an olive.
4. Divide the watercress into sixteen equal portions and arrange them in the
   spaces between the eggs, with the stems pointing inwards.
5. Mix the radishes, green pepper, and carrots together in a bowl.
6. Pile the mixture into the middle of the ring made by the eggs.
7. Combine all the ingredients for the sauce together in a small bowl and beat
   thoroughly.
8. Pour into a sauce boat and serve with the salad.

gardofilov aghtsan

POTATO AND YOGURT APPETIZER

A recipe from the Caucasus, popular with Armenians and Georgians, this dish is traditionally made with sour cream, but I have adapted it to use yogurt. It makes a fine appetizer or side salad.

1½ lb (¾ kg) evenly sized potatoes
½ cucumber, peeled and thinly
  sliced
2 shallots, finely chopped, or 2
  scallions, finely sliced

1 teaspoon salt
½ teaspoon black pepper
generous ½ cup (150 ml) yogurt
2 tablespoons finely chopped
  parsley

1. Wash the potatoes and cook in boiling water.
2. When tender, drain, cool, and peel.
3. Cut the potatoes into ½ in (1 cm) pieces and place in a large salad bowl.
4. Add the cucumber slices and chopped onion.
5. Gently stir in the salt, pepper, and yogurt and leave in the refrigerator for an hour.
6. Serve sprinkled with the chopped parsley.

borani-ye-esfenag

IRANIAN SPINACH AND YOGURT SALAD

A simple, cheap, and appetizing salad. It is related to the Armenian *shomin*, but here the yogurt is tossed into the salad proper and it is served chilled. It is also an excellent accompaniment to meat dishes.

½ lb (250 g) spinach
2 tablespoons lemon juice
1 tablespoon finely chopped onion
½ teaspoon salt

a pinch of black pepper
1¼ cups (300 ml) yogurt
1 tablespoon finely chopped fresh
   mint or 1 teaspoon dried mint

1. Wash the spinach several times in cold water.
2. Strip the leaves from the stalks and discard the stalks.
3. In a large saucepan, bring 2½ cups (½ l) water to a boil.
4. Add the spinach, lower the heat, and simmer for about 10 minutes.
5. Drain the spinach in a colander, allow to cool a little, then squeeze out any remaining water.
6. Finely chop the spinach and put it into a large salad bowl.
7. Add the lemon juice, onion, salt, and pepper.
8. Toss with a wooden spoon.
9. Add the yogurt and mix thoroughly.
10. Refrigerate for at least an hour.
11. Serve with a garnish of mint.

bulz gătiti cu ouă

FRIED DUMPLINGS FILLED WITH BUTTER AND CHEESE

This is a classic Romanian dish made with polenta (cornmeal), which is also popular in Italian cuisine. Although usually served with sour cream, try topping them with yogurt instead. They are a little difficult to make, but you will find that they will be worth the effort. They can be served as a starter or as a light main course.

6 oz (175 g) polenta
1½ teaspoons salt
6 x ½ in (1 cm) cubes hard butter
6 x ½ in (1 cm) cubes strong,

hard cheese, e.g. halloumi, Cheddar, or Parmesan
4 tablespoons (2 oz/50 g) butter
1¼ cups (300 ml) yogurt

1. Put the polenta and salt into a large saucepan with 2½ cups (600 ml) water.
2. Bring to a boil, stirring continuously, and cook for a further 5 to 8 minutes, still stirring, until the mixture is very thick.
3. Pour the mixture on to a plate and leave until it is completely cold.
4. Divide the mixture into six and flatten with your hands into cakes roughly round in shape.
5. Put a cube of butter and a cube of cheese into the center of each.
6. Wet your hands and then shape each cake into a round dumpling, making sure that the filling is completely enclosed.
7. Heat the grill to red hot and then melt 4 tablespoons (2 oz/50 g) butter in the grill pan.
8. Place the dumplings in the pan and roll them in the butter until completely coated.
9. Grill for about 10 minutes, turning once.
10. Serve immediately with any remaining butter in the grill pan poured over the dumplings; top with the yogurt.

shrimp cocktail with yogurt

The ever-popular shrimp cocktail with a difference. The flavor of yogurt gives it a new dimension.

1¼ cups (300 ml) yogurt
2-3 tablespoons mayonnaise
½ teaspoon salt
¼ teaspoon black pepper
lettuce leaves, washed, dried, and
  finely shredded

1 tablespoon tomato paste
a few drops tabasco
1 lb (½ kg) shrimp—if frozen
  thaw them out
lemon wedges

1. In a bowl mix the yogurt, mayonnaise, tomato paste, tabasco, salt, and pepper, and chill in the refrigerator.
2. When ready to serve, arrange shredded lettuce in individual bowls or plates and place the shrimp on top.
3. Spoon the yogurt sauce over the shrimp.
4. Serve a large lemon wedge with each portion.

laban-bi-tahina

YOGURT WITH SESAME SEED PASTE

A popular Arab dish made of sesame seed paste and yogurt. It is served with thin bread as an appetizer, or as an accompaniment to grilled fish or meat.

1¼ cups (300 ml) *tahina*
2 garlic cloves, crushed
½ teaspoon salt
1¼ cups (300 ml) yogurt

juice of 2 lemons
pinch of ground cumin
pinch of paprika
1 tablespoon finely chopped parsley

1. Pour the *tahina* into a bowl, add the garlic and salt, and mix well.
2. Add the yogurt and lemon juice and then beat vigorously for several minutes until you have a thick, smooth cream.
3. Pour into a shallow bowl and sprinkle decoratively with the golden cumin and red paprika.
4. Garnish with the parsley, either scattered all over the surface or bunched together in the center.

salted herring with yogurt

This is a recipe from Irfan Orga's book *Cooking with Yogurt*. It makes a marvelous hors d'oeuvre.

4 salted herring fillets
6 soft herring roes
1 tablespoon tarragon vinegar
6 tablespoons yogurt

½ teaspoon finely chopped onion
½ teaspoon chervil
½ teaspoon chives
½ teaspoon tarragon

1. Soak the herring fillets in cold water for an hour and then drain.
2. Arrange them on a large serving dish.
3. In a small bowl, mash the roes with the vinegar and yogurt.
4. Stir in the onion and herbs.
5. Pour this mixture over the herring and chill until ready to serve.

salads

asbourag aghtsan

ASPARAGUS AND YOGURT SALAD

This is an old recipe dating from the tenth century. It is a highly sophisticated combination of asparagus and yogurt with the added flavor of garlic.

1 lb (½ kg) fresh asparagus
1½ teaspoons salt
2 cups (500 ml) yogurt
1 teaspoon dried mint

1–2 garlic cloves (depending
  on taste), crushed
1 scallion, finely sliced
1 hard-boiled egg, chopped

1. Remove the tough white part at the bottom of each asparagus stalk.
   You will achieve a more even effect if you cut them rather than snap them off.
2. Cut stalks roughly into 1 in (3 cm) pieces.
3. Put into a large saucepan, just cover with water, add 1 teaspoon of salt,
   and bring to a boil.
4. Simmer for about 5 minutes or until just tender. Be careful not to overcook.
5. Drain the asparagus and leave to cool.
6. Pour the yogurt into a small bowl and stir in the garlic, ½ teaspoon salt,
   mint, and onion. Stir until well blended.
7. Gently stir the chopped egg through the sauce.
8. Place the asparagus in a serving bowl and spoon the sauce over the top.
9. Serve cold with roast meat or poultry or cold cuts.

baigan pachchadi

SPICED EGGPLANT WITH YOGURT

This dish comes from north India, where there are several such vegetable dishes cooked with mustard seeds, chilis, and yogurt. Zucchini, okra, spinach, turnips, etc. can be substituted for the eggplant. Serve with meat and poultry dishes as well as with dry curry dishes.

3 tablespoons oil
1 teaspoon black mustard seeds
1 onion, finely chopped
2 fresh green chilis, seeded
  and sliced
1 medium eggplant, peeled
  and diced

1 tomato, chopped
1 teaspoon salt
1 teaspoon *garam masala*
½ teaspoon chili powder (optional)
1¼ cups (300 ml) yogurt
2 tablespoons chopped
  fresh cilantro

1. Heat the oil in a saucepan and fry the mustard seeds until they pop.
2. Add the onions and chilis, and fry until the onion is soft.
3. Add the eggplant and fry for a few minutes, stirring frequently.
4. Stir in the tomato, salt, *garam masala*, and chili powder.
5. Add ¼ cup (60 ml) water, stir well, cover, and cook until the eggplant and tomato can be mashed to a purée.
6. Cool; stir in the yogurt and half of the chopped cilantro.
7. Serve garnished with the remaining cilantro.

madzna-gaghamp

CABBAGE AND OLIVE SALAD WITH YOGURT

This is my adaptation of an Armenian salad. The white cabbage is traditionally pickled in a marinade for several days until it turns red. You can use red cabbage but it will lack the sharp, biting flavor of marinated cabbage.

¾ lb (350 g) cabbage, preferably
   pickled (see p. 90)
1 onion, finely chopped
2 apples, peeled, cored, and cut into
   small cubes
a small bunch of grapes, separated
   and washed
20 black olives, pitted and halved

2 tablespoons walnuts,
   coarsely chopped
1 teaspoon salt
1¼ cups (300 ml) yogurt
1 teaspoon oregano
fresh tarragon or watercress
   as a garnish

1. Coarsely chop the cabbage leaves.
2. Place the cabbage in a large bowl together with the onion, apples, grapes, olives, walnuts, and salt.
3. Toss the salad lightly and chill for at least 1 hour.
4. To serve the salad, arrange it in a pyramid shape on a flat plate.
5. Whisk the yogurt until it is frothy.
6. Pour the yogurt over the salad.
7. Sprinkle the oregano over the top and garnish with the tarragon or watercress.

madzounov shaghgam

BEET AND YOGURT SALAD

This Armenian salad is popular throughout the Caucasus and northern Iran.
It makes a good accompaniment to roast meats and chicken.

1 lb (½ kg) beets, washed; remove
  the tops but do not cut the skin
  (or use canned beets)
2 tablespoons (1 oz/25 g) butter

1 onion, finely chopped
1¼ cups (300 ml) garlic yogurt sauce
  (see p. 247)

1. Cook the beets in lightly-salted boiling water for about 1 hour or until tender.
2. Drain, dip in cold water, and rub off the skins.
3. Melt the butter in a small saucepan and sauté the onion until golden brown.
4. Dice the beets and add to the saucepan.
5. Keep warm until ready to serve.
6. Arrange in a dish and pour the yogurt sauce over the top.

A GREEK VARIATION

1. Follow the above recipe up to the end of step 4.
2. Stir in the garlic yogurt sauce, 3 tablespoons white wine, and 1 teaspoon sugar.
3. Heat through but do not boil.
4. Spoon into a serving dish and sprinkle with a little chopped parsley.

AN ARABIC VARIATION

Here the butter and onion are omitted and the diced beet is tossed in lemon juice
and olive oil and then garnished with a little chopped parsley.

avocado im egozim

AVOCADO AND WALNUT SALAD

This Israeli salad uses avocado, walnuts, and yogurt, which, strange as it may seem, go very well together. It is an ideal accompaniment to all kinds of roast or grilled meats.

2 ripe avocados
juice of 1 lime (or lemon)
4 scallions, finely sliced,
   including green parts
2 dill pickles, thinly sliced
generous ½ cup (150 ml) yogurt—
   or more depending on taste

1 celery stick, finely chopped
2 oz (50 g) walnuts, chopped
1 teaspoon salt
¼ teaspoon black pepper
2 tablespoons chopped parsley
½ teaspoon dill
24 black olives

1. Cut the avocados in half, lengthwise; remove the pits and carefully scoop out the flesh.
2. Cube the flesh and place in a large salad bowl.
3. Sprinkle with the lime or lemon juice and add the scallions, dill pickles, celery, and walnuts.
4. Season with the salt, pepper, and parsley, and toss.
5. Stir in the yogurt and then refrigerate for at least 1 hour.
6. Before serving, sprinkle with the dill and garnish with the black olives.

pickled cabbage

If you would like to pickle cabbage in the Armenian way then try this simple method.

1. Put the cabbage into a large saucepan or casserole and cover with cold water.
2. Bring to a boil and simmer for about 45 minutes or until tender.
3. Drain and chop the leaves coarsely.
4. Put the cabbage in a large bowl, preferably glass or earthenware, and add:

2 lb (1 kg) beets, peeled and cubed
a few sprigs parsley
1 bunch green celery leaves
2½ cups (600 ml) wine vinegar

2 teaspoons paprika
sufficient water to cover
  by 2–3 in (5–8 cm)

5. Place a plate with a weight on it over the cabbage to keep it under the marinade. If the weight is metal it should be wrapped in foil.
6. Leave to pickle for 1 week.
7. By the end of the week the cabbage will have turned deep red and have a piquant flavor.

garosi aghtsan

CELERY AND WALNUTS WITH SWEET YOGURT

This Caucasian salad is a good accompaniment to pork or poultry roasts and kebabs. If you cannot find quinces use apples instead.

3 sticks celery
2 quinces or 3 apples
1¼ cups (300 ml) yogurt
2 tablespoons runny honey

2 tablespoons chopped walnuts
a few drops lemon juice
1 tablespoon chopped parsley

1. Wash the celery thoroughly and cut into ¼ in (½ cm) pieces.
2. Peel and core the quinces or apples and chop them into ½ in (1 cm) cubes.
3. Pour the yogurt into a bowl and whisk until frothy; add the honey and continue whisking.
4. Sprinkle the walnuts into the yogurt.
5. Arrange the celery and quinces in a serving bowl and pour the yogurt sauce over them.
6. Sprinkle with lemon juice and chopped parsley and serve.

VARIATION

Grated carrots and apples with yogurt and honey dressing also makes a tasty salad. Use the same quantities and method as above.

biberli cacuk

YOGURT AND PEPPER SALAD

A regional speciality from Marisa, Turkey. The quantities are the same as for the popular *jajig* (see p. 92) but substitute 3 tablespoons finely chopped parsley for the mint and omit the chili powder.

1. Grill 6 small green hot peppers, turning twice. Allow to cool, peel off the skin, and remove the seeds.
2. Cut the peppers into ¼ in (½ cm) cubes.
3. Place the yogurt in a mixing bowl.
4. Stir in salt, garlic, chopped peppers, 3 tablespoons finely chopped parsley, and 1 thinly sliced garlic clove. Mix well.
5. Serve in individual side dishes with 1 teaspoon of olive oil on top.

jajig

CUCUMBER AND YOGURT SALAD WITH GARLIC AND SALT

Çaçuk in Turkey, *tzajiki* in Greece and the Balkans, *mast-khiar* in Iran, *khira raita* in India, *khiar-bi-laban* in Arab lands, and *jajig* in Armenia, this is perhaps the best known yogurt-based salad of all. Simple and versatile, it can be served with any dish. If you add 2½ cups (½ l) water to it, you get a cool, refreshing soup.

2½ cups (½ l) yogurt
½ teaspoon salt
1 garlic clove, crushed
1 cucumber, peeled and diced

1 tablespoon finely chopped fresh
   mint or 1 teaspoon dried mint
a pinch of chili powder as a garnish

1. Place the yogurt in a mixing bowl.
2. Stir in the salt, garlic, cucumber, and mint and mix well.
3. Place in the refrigerator to chill until ready to serve.
4. Pour into individual side dishes and sprinkle with the chili powder.

vellarikai pachchadi

INDIAN CUCUMBER AND YOGURT SALAD

This may be served as an accompaniment to any curry. If fresh coconut is not available, use dried shredded coconut soaked in half the yogurt for 30 minutes and then blend in as directed. It is a rather hot salad—be warned!

1 cucumber, peeled and finely
   chopped
½ fresh coconut or 1 oz (25 g) dried
   shredded coconut
2 green chilis, seeded

2 cups (450 ml) yogurt
1 teaspoon salt
2 teaspoons vegetable oil
1 teaspoon mustard seeds

1. Place the chopped cucumber in a colander and set aside to drain for 1 hour.
2. With a sharp knife, pare off the thin brown skin of the coconut and cut the flesh into pieces.
3. Put the coconut pieces and chilis into a blender.
4. Add 2 to 3 tablespoons of water and blend until a smooth purée is formed.
5. Add more water if necessary.
6. Scrape the purée into a medium-sized serving bowl.
7. Beat in the yogurt, cucumber, and salt.
8. In a small frying pan, heat the oil and fry the mustard seeds until they pop.
9. Stir the mustard seeds and the oil into the yogurt mixture.
10. Cover the bowl and chill until ready to serve.

kela raeta

BANANA IN YOGURT

Very good with meat and chicken curries.

2 cups (½ l) yogurt
3 bananas, thinly sliced
½ teaspoon salt

1 green chili, finely chopped
2 teaspoons finely chopped
   cilantro or parsley

1. Beat the yogurt with salt, until smooth.
2. Add the bananas and chili.
3. Cover the mixture and chill.
4. Before serving, sprinkle with the cilantro or parsley.

mango raeta

MANGOES IN YOGURT

From northern India, this salad can be served with curries, roasts, and grilled meats. *Raeta* means "vegetable with curd" and virtually any fruit or vegetable can be prepared in this way. The more popular ones are banana, cucumber, onion, potato, eggplant, and mango—the recipe for which is given below.

2½ cups (½ l) yogurt
2 ripe, fresh mangoes, peeled,
    pitted, and diced (if fresh
    mangoes are not available, use
    canned)
½ teaspoon salt

1 tablespoon ghee or clarified butter
1 tablespoon mustard seeds
1 green chili, finely chopped
2 teaspoons finely chopped cilantro
    or parsley

1. In a mixing bowl, beat the yogurt until smooth.
2. Add the mangoes and salt, stir and set aside.
3. In a small pan, melt the ghee. When it is hot, add the mustard seeds and fry until they begin to pop.
4. Add the chili and fry, stirring constantly, for 10 seconds.
5. Tip the contents of the pan into the yogurt mixture and stir well.
6. Cover the mixture and chill.
7. Before serving sprinkle with the cilantro or parsley.

narinchi aghtsan

ARMENIAN ORANGE SALAD

This is a tangy salad of oranges and dates. It looks extremely decorative on a buffet table and is a refreshing accompaniment to any poultry dish.

4 oranges
10 dates, pitted and chopped
1 tablespoon slivered almonds
1 tablespoon superfine sugar

juice of 1 lemon
⅓ cup (75 ml) yogurt
⅓ cup (75 ml) heavy cream
a pinch of cinnamon

1. Peel the oranges, removing as much of the white pith as possible.
2. Slice them thinly, crosswise.
3. Arrange the slices over a large platter.
4. Scatter the chopped dates and the almonds over the oranges.
5. In a small bowl mix together the sugar, lemon juice, yogurt, and cream.
6. Pour this sauce over the salad, sprinkle with the cinnamon, and serve.

portakal salatasi

ORANGE AND YOGURT SALAD

This is an adaptation of an Ottoman salad popular throughout what was the Ottoman Empire. The use of orange liqueur, chocolate-orange liqueur, or other citrus liqueur is optional but it adds a new and interesting flavor. Try this salad with roast lamb or chicken.

2 large oranges
1 small head lettuce
¼ head curly endive

3 tablespoons superfine sugar
2 tablespoons citrus liqueur
generous ½ cup (150 ml) yogurt

1. Peel the oranges and slice them very thinly, crosswise.
2. Wash the lettuce leaves and endive, pat dry with paper towels, and arrange in a salad bowl.

3. Now arrange the orange slices decoratively around the center of the bowl.
4. Sprinkle the oranges with the sugar and liqueur and then place the salad in the refrigerator for at least 2 hours.
5. Just before serving, beat the yogurt until smooth and spoon it over the salad.

salade sib zamini ba mast

POTATO SALAD WITH YOGURT

Most of the salads now popular in Iran are European in origin, although over the years they have been adapted to local tastes and ingredients. This salad is no exception. It is based on the Russian sour cream and potato salad.

3–4 large potatoes
1¼ cups (300 ml) yogurt
generous ½ cup (150 ml) sour cream
   (or use more yogurt instead)
1 teaspoon salt
1 tablespoon fresh dill
   or 1 teaspoon dried dill

½ teaspoon black pepper
3 hard-boiled eggs, peeled
   and chopped
4 large dill pickles or ½ fresh
   cucumber, thinly sliced
fresh tarragon as a garnish
   (optional)

1. Cook the potatoes in a large pot of boiling water until tender.
2. Allow to cool; peel and cut into small cubes.
3. In a small bowl, mix the yogurt and sour cream together, then stir in the salt, black pepper, and dill.
4. Put the chopped potatoes, eggs, and dill pickles or fresh cucumber into a large salad bowl.
5. Pour the dressing over the top and then stir gently.
6. Garnish and place in the refrigerator for at least 1 hour before serving.

VARIATION
You can also try cubed cooked potatoes dressed with yogurt mayonnaise (p. 248), horseradish sauce (p. 246), and herbs.

palak raeta

SPINACH WITH YOGURT AND SPICES

One of the splendid Indian *raetas*, or yogurt-based salads; this dish makes an
exciting use of spices. Serve chilled or at room temperature as an accompaniment
to any curry or kebab.

1 lb (½ kg) spinach, fresh or frozen
1 tablespoon ghee or vegetable oil
1 teaspoon black mustard seeds
1 teaspoon cumin seeds
1 teaspoon ground cumin

½ teaspoon fenugreek seeds
½ teaspoon chili powder
1 teaspoon salt
1¼ cups (300 ml) yogurt

1. If using fresh spinach, wash thoroughly. Place in a saucepan with sufficient
   boiling water to cover and simmer for about 10 minutes.
2. If using frozen spinach, thaw and simmer in boiling water for 5 to 10 minutes
   until tender.
3. Drain the spinach and squeeze out any remaining water.
4. Chop the spinach.
5. Heat the ghee or oil in a saucepan and fry the mustard seeds until they pop.
6. Add the cumin seeds, ground cumin, and the fenugreek, and continue
   to fry, stirring frequently.
7. When the fenugreek seeds turn a brownish color, remove the pan from
   the heat.
8. Stir in the chili powder and salt and allow to cool.
9. Add the yogurt to the spice mixture and stir well.
10. Place the spinach in a serving bowl, pour the yogurt over the top,
    and stir well.

watercress and radish salad

I have found this salad with its cinnamon yogurt dressing very successful with grilled fish and fish dishes generally.

1 head romaine lettuce
1 bunch watercress
12 radishes

1¼ cups (300 ml) cinnamon yogurt
   sauce (see p. 246)
juice of ½ lemon

1. Remove any coarse lettuce leaves and wash the remaining ones carefully.
2. Trim and wash the watercress.
3. Pat the lettuce and watercress dry on paper towels.
4. Wash the radishes; trim and slice thinly.
5. Shred the lettuce leaves finely and place in a salad bowl.
6. Add the watercress and the radishes.
7. Pour the cinnamon yogurt sauce over the salad, together with the lemon juice.
8. Toss well and chill for at least an hour before serving.

surki aghtsan

SPICED DRIED YOGURT SALAD

This is an Armenian salad from the mountains of Cilicia. It is one of the great classics of the region. I regard this as one of the most exciting and unusual salads I have ever tasted.

1 *surki* ball (see p. 21)
4 tomatoes, thinly sliced
4 in (10 cm) piece of cucumber,
   halved lengthwise and
   thinly sliced

1 small onion, thinly sliced
2 tablespoons finely chopped
   parsley
2 tablespoons olive oil
juice of ½ lemon

1. Break the *surki* ball into ½ in (1 cm) pieces with a sharp knife.
2. In a large bowl mix the sliced tomatoes, cucumber, onion, and chopped parsley.
3. Add the *surki* pieces, olive oil, and lemon juice, and mix well.
4. Serve on its own or as an accompaniment to any roast meat.

shominov tzoo

SPINACH AND EGG SALAD

An unusual salad of fresh spinach and yogurt combined to create a unique flavor.
Serve with roast or grilled meat or poultry.

½ lb (250 g) fresh spinach leaves
4 scallions, including the green
   tops, finely sliced
1–2 cups (300–450 ml) yogurt
¼ cup (60 ml) olive oil
1 teaspoon salt

½ teaspoon black pepper
4 hard-boiled eggs, peeled
   and chopped
about 15 black olives
pinch of paprika

1. Wash the spinach leaves very thoroughly.
2. Drain the leaves, pat dry with paper towels, and then shred.
3. In a large salad bowl, combine and mix the shredded leaves and the scallions.
4. In a small bowl, blend the yogurt, olive oil, salt, and pepper.
5. Stir in the chopped eggs.
6. Pour this mixture over the spinach and toss carefully so as not to
   break up the eggs too much.
7. Garnish with black olives and sprinkle paprika over the top.
8. Serve chilled.

salata bi laban

ARAB MIXED SALAD

Popular in Egypt and Syria, this fresh, mixed salad receives extra flavor from the addition of yogurt. It gives the vegetables a cool, tangy delicacy. Serve with kebabs, or other meat dishes.

1 green pepper, thinly sliced
1 onion, finely sliced
4 tomatoes, sliced
1 garlic clove, crushed
1 tablespoon finely chopped parsley
4–5 coriander seeds, crushed, or
  ½ teaspoon ground coriander

juice of 1 lemon
3 tablespoons olive oil
1 tablespoon chopped fresh mint
  or 1 teaspoon dried mint
1 teaspoon salt
½ teaspoon black pepper
1¼ cups (300 ml) yogurt

1. Put the sliced pepper, onion, and tomatoes into a large salad bowl together with all the other ingredients, apart from the yogurt.
2. Mix all the ingredients together and set aside until ready to serve.
3. Just before serving, pour the yogurt over the salad, and mix.

zeytov surki

SPICED DRIED YOGURT WITH OLIVES

A Cilician–Armenian salad dating from ancient times; simple and tasty. It is excellent on its own with hot pita bread or *lavash* and *tan*—a yogurt drink (see p. 256).

1 *surki* ball (see p. 21)
1 small onion, thinly sliced

some black olives
½ teaspoon chili pepper

1. Slice a ball of *surki* thinly.
2. Add the onion and toss gently.
3. Arrange on a plate and garnish with the olives and pepper.

bistagov-khozi aghtsan

PISTACHIO AND HAM SALAD

This is a recipe of mine based on a traditional Armenian one of pistachios, sour cream, and shredded chicken breasts. I find that chopped ham with salted pistachios gives more exciting results. Halloumi cheese can be bought from most gourmet stores. It is slightly salty.

SERVES SIX

6 oz (175 g) halloumi cheese
  (use Cheddar if you prefer)
4 small apples
1 lb (½ kg) cooked ham cut into
  ½ in (1 cm) pieces (or cooked
  chicken breasts, shredded)
½ lb (250 g) celery cut into ¼ in
  (½ cm) slices

2 scallions, including green parts,
  sliced into ¼ in (½ cm) pieces
6 oz (175 g) shelled pistachios
2½ cups (600 ml) yogurt
  mayonnaise (see p. 248)
juice of 1 lemon
1 teaspoon salt
½ teaspoon cayenne pepper
1 teaspoon turmeric

1. Wash the halloumi under cold running water to remove the brine and then cut into ½ in (1 cm) cubes.
2. Peel the apples, remove the cores, and cut into ½ in (1 cm) cubes.
3. In a large bowl, toss together the cheese, apples, ham (or chicken), celery, scallions, and pistachios.
4. Pour the yogurt mayonnaise over the salad, together with the lemon juice, salt, and cayenne pepper. Mix well.
5. Allow to chill for an hour or so.
6. Garnish with the turmeric and serve.

egg and yogurt salad

This simple egg salad can be a meal on its own, as well as making an excellent accompaniment to roast chicken or beef.

DRESSING

1¼ cups (300 ml) yogurt
1 teaspoon paprika
1 teaspoon sugar
1 tablespoon lemon juice
1 tablespoon orange juice
¼ teaspoon black pepper
1 tablespoon finely chopped parsley

SALAD

4 sticks celery, washed and
    finely sliced
4 hard-boiled eggs, peeled
    and sliced
2 carrots, peeled and grated
8 radishes, washed, trimmed,
    and finely sliced
½ cucumber, sliced

1. First prepare the dressing by combining all its ingredients in a large bowl.
2. Set half the dressing aside and fold the celery through the remaining dressing.
3. Spoon the celery into a salad bowl.
4. Arrange the egg slices over the celery and then cover with grated carrot.
5. Surround the edges of the bowl with the sliced radishes and cucumber.
6. Spoon the remaining dressing over the top.
7. Chill for about 30 minutes and serve.

mast-e-khiar

LABNA WITH VEGETABLES AND NUTS

This slightly more elaborate version of *labna* is Iranian by origin. It is one of those dishes that is sometimes eaten as an appetizer, sometimes as a salad accompanying roast meats, and sometimes as a meal in itself.

2½ cups (600 ml) yogurt
1 cucumber, peeled and finely
  chopped
1 onion, grated
1 tablespoon finely chopped fresh
  mint or 1 teaspoon dried mint
2 oz (50 g) walnuts, chopped

2 teaspoons salt
½ tablespoon fresh dill
  or ½ teaspoon dried dill
2 oz (50 g) currants
4 radishes, washed, trimmed, and
  finely chopped
washed lettuce leaves as a garnish

1. Use the yogurt to prepare *labna* as described on p. 18.
2. Turn the *labna* into a mixing bowl and add all the remaining ingredients except the radishes and lettuce leaves.
3. Mix the ingredients together.
4. Shape the mixture into small balls. Use a melon baller if you have one.
5. Arrange the lettuce leaves around a large plate, place the balls of *mast-e-khiar* in the center, and sprinkle the chopped radishes over the top.

vegetable dishes

baigan dahi

EGGPLANT WITH YOGURT

An Indian dish that can be served as a snack with bread and fresh vegetables or as an accompaniment to curries and pilafs. Cheap, simple, and tasty.

2 medium eggplants
3 tablespoons cooking oil
2 onions, finely chopped
3 garlic cloves, finely chopped
2 teaspoons finely grated
  fresh ginger
2 teaspoons ground coriander

1 teaspoon ground cumin
½ teaspoon turmeric
½ teaspoon chili powder
1½ teaspoons salt
½ teaspoon *garam masala*
2 teaspoons sugar, optional
1¼ cups (300 ml) yogurt

1. Place the eggplants under a hot broiler or in a hot oven and cook until the flesh is soft throughout.
2. Leave until cool enough to handle, peel, and either finely chop or mash the flesh.
3. Heat the oil in a saucepan and fry the onions, garlic, and ginger until the onions are soft and golden.
4. Add the coriander, cumin, turmeric, and chili powder and fry, stirring, for another minute.
5. Stir in the salt and add the chopped or mashed eggplant.
6. Stir and cook for a few minutes then sprinkle with the *garam masala*. Cover, and cook for 5 minutes longer.
7. Taste and adjust seasoning if necessary. You can also add the sugar now, if using.
8. Beat the yogurt until smooth and stir into the eggplants before serving.

siserov letsonadz sumpoog

EGGPLANT STUFFED WITH CHICKPEAS

This Armenian dish can be served as an appetizer or as a light vegetarian main course. It is a popular dish for Lent.

½ lb (250 g) dried chickpeas, soaked overnight in cold water
4 medium eggplants
4 tablespoons (2 oz/50 g) ghee or butter
1 onion, finely chopped
1 garlic clove, finely chopped
1 tablespoon tomato paste

1 teaspoon marjoram
1 teaspoon salt
½ teaspoon chili powder
2 tablespoons chopped parsley
vegetable oil for frying
1¼ cups (300 ml) yogurt herb dressing (see p. 250)

1. Rinse the chickpeas under cold running water.
2. Place them in a large saucepan three-quarters filled with water and bring to a boil. Spoon off any scum that comes to the surface.
3. Reduce heat and simmer vigorously for about 1 hour or until the chickpeas are tender. It may be necessary to add more boiling water.
4. Drain in a colander, rinse under cold water, and set aside until cool enough to handle.
5. Meanwhile, cut the heads off the eggplants. Using an apple corer, remove most of the flesh and seeds, being careful not to damage the outer shells.
6. Half-fill a large pan with water and bring to a boil, add the eggplants, and simmer for 10 minutes.
7. Drain the eggplants and set aside.
8. Meanwhile, by pressing each chickpea between thumb and forefinger, remove its skin and discard.
9. Melt the butter in a large frying pan, add the onion and garlic, and sauté until golden brown.
10. Stir in the tomato paste, marjoram, salt, chili powder, chickpeas, and 1 tablespoon of the parsley.

11. Cook for a few minutes and then set aside.
12. Fill the cavity of each eggplant with the chickpea mixture.
13. Pour a generous ½ cup (150 ml) vegetable oil into a large frying pan and heat.
14. Add the eggplants and fry gently for 10 to 15 minutes, turning carefully from time to time, until cooked through.
15. Serve sprinkled with the remaining parsley and accompanied by the yogurt herb dressing.

kharapakhi lobi madznov

GREEN BEANS WITH YOGURT SAUCE

This dish is traditionally made with sour cream and tomatoes but this simpler version uses only yogurt. Serve as a side dish to meat or poultry dishes, or on its own with bread and pickles.

1 lb (½ kg) green beans, trimmed
 and halved crosswise
4 tablespoons (2 oz/50 g) butter
1 onion, finely chopped
1 green pepper, seeds and white
 pith removed and discarded,
 sliced thinly

1 tablespoon chopped fresh basil
 or 1 teaspoon dried basil
2 cups (450 ml) garlic yogurt sauce
 (see p. 247)
1 tablespoon finely chopped parsley

1. Half-fill a large pan with lightly-salted water and bring to a boil.
2. Add the beans and boil for about 10 minutes or until they are tender but still firm.
3. Drain and set aside.
4. Melt the butter in a large frying pan, add the onion and green pepper, and sauté until soft.
5. Stir in the beans and basil and simmer for a further 2 to 3 minutes.
6. Spoon the mixture into a serving dish, pour the garlic yogurt sauce over the top, and sprinkle with the parsley.

beets with yogurt sauce

An Arabic dish that makes a good accompaniment to roast chicken or grilled fish.

2 tablespoons (1 oz/25 g) butter
2 oz (50 g) flour
1¼ cups (300 ml) chicken stock
1 small onion, finely chopped
½ teaspoon dried dill
½ teaspoon salt

¼ teaspoon white pepper
generous ½ cup (150 ml) yogurt
6 medium-sized beets, cooked,
   peeled, and thinly sliced
1 tablespoon chopped parsley

1. Melt the butter in a saucepan.
2. Stir in the flour and cook for 1 minute.
3. Remove the pan from the heat and slowly pour in the stock, stirring constantly.
4. When the sauce is smooth, return the pan to the heat.
5. Stirring continuously, bring the sauce to a boil and cook for 5 minutes or until the sauce has thickened.
6. Add the onion, dill, salt and pepper, and cook for 5 to 10 minutes until the onion is soft.
7. Put the yogurt into a small bowl and stir in 2 tablespoons of the hot sauce.
8. Now pour the mixture back into the sauce.
9. Gently mix in the beet slices. Make sure that all the slices are covered with the sauce.
10. Leave over a very low heat for 2 to 3 minutes to heat through but do not boil.
11. Pour the beets and sauce into a serving dish, sprinkle with chopped parsley, and serve hot.

brussels sprouts in yogurt

I like this vegetable dish very much. It is one of Irfan Orga's (from *Cooking with Yogurt*) and is a most original accompaniment to any roast meat.

2 lb (1 kg) Brussels sprouts, rough outer leaves removed and a slit made in the base of each stalk
1 tablespoon (½ oz/15 g) butter
2 large tomatoes, blanched, skinned, and chopped
2 teaspoons chopped fresh chives or

1 teaspoon dried chives
salt and pepper to taste
¼ teaspoon ground nutmeg
1¼ cups (300 ml) yogurt, stabilized (see p. 17)
1 oz (25 g) grated Parmesan cheese
1 oz (25 g) toasted, slivered almonds

1. Bring a large saucepan half filled with slightly-salted water to a boil.
2. Add the sprouts and simmer until they are just tender.
3. Preheat the oven to 350°F (180°C).
4. Drain the sprouts in a colander.
5. Butter a casserole dish and empty the sprouts into it.
6. Arrange the chopped tomatoes over the top and sprinkle with the chives.
7. Season with the salt, pepper, and nutmeg.
8. Beat the yogurt until smooth and pour over the vegetables.
9. Sprinkle with the cheese and bake for about 20 minutes or until golden brown.
10. Scatter the toasted almonds over the top and serve.

boiled cabbage with yogurt

Traditionally this Hungarian/Romanian vegetable dish is made with sour cream. I have substituted yogurt and it is delicious. It is usually served with roast pork, but goes well with lamb and beef as well.

1 firm white cabbage (2–3 lb/ 1–1½ kg)
4 tablespoons (2 oz/50 g) butter
1 small onion, finely chopped
2 teaspoons salt
1 teaspoon caraway seeds

1 teaspoon dried mint or 1 tablespoon chopped fresh mint
1¼ cups (300 ml) yogurt
1 garlic clove, crushed
ground black pepper, to taste

1. Remove the coarse outer leaves of the cabbage, cut into quarters, and remove the hard central core.
2. Cut the cabbage into narrow strips, wash, and drain.
3. Melt the butter in a large saucepan and sauté the onion until it is soft but not brown.
4. Add the chopped cabbage together with the salt, caraway seeds, mint, and just sufficient water to prevent the cabbage from sticking while cooking.
5. Simmer until the cabbage is just tender, stirring occasionally.
6. Pour the yogurt into a small bowl and whisk in the garlic.
7. Pour this mixture over the cabbage, stir, and heat through but do not boil.
8. Turn into a serving dish, sprinkle with black pepper, and serve.

tzvov tutmig

FRIED ZUCCHINI IN YOGURT

Yogurt has a great affinity with fried vegetables. You can use eggplant, mushrooms, or tomatoes instead of zucchini.

4 large zucchinis
1–2 garlic cloves, crushed
1 teaspoon salt
1 teaspoon dried dill
1 teaspoon dried mint

2 eggs
vegetable oil for frying
1¼ cups (300 ml) yogurt
1 tablespoon finely chopped parsley

1. Wash the zucchinis, remove heads and tails, and cut into ¼ in (½ cm) slices.
2. Half-fill a saucepan with slightly-salted water and bring to a boil.
3. Add the zucchini slices and cook until just tender.
4. Strain in a colander.
5. Break the eggs into a bowl, add the garlic, salt, dill, and mint, and beat with a fork.
6. Heat a little of the oil in a large frying pan.
7. Dip some of the zucchini slices in the egg and place in the pan.
8. Fry on both sides until golden.
9. Remove to a serving dish and keep warm while you cook the remaining slices in the same way.
10. Pour the yogurt over the top and sprinkle with the parsley.
11. Serve warm with roast meats or cold as an appetizer.

yogourtlu havuç salatasi

FRIED CARROTS IN YOGURT

This is a popular Turkish and Balkan dish that goes well with grilled and roasted lamb or beef.

1 lb (½ kg) carrots, peeled or
   scraped and washed
2 tablespoons flour
3 tablespoons olive oil
1 teaspoon salt

½ teaspoon ground white pepper
½ teaspoon caraway seeds
1¼ cups (300 ml) yogurt
1 tablespoon chopped fresh mint
   or 1 teaspoon dried mint

1. Chop the carrots into ¼ in (½ cm) slices.
2. Cook in boiling salted water for 10 to 15 minutes or until tender.
3. Drain and dry thoroughly on paper towels.
4. Toss the carrots in the flour.
5. Heat the oil in a large frying pan, add the floured carrots, and cook, turning occasionally, until browned on both sides.
6. Add the salt, pepper, and caraway seeds, and stir well.
7. Warm the yogurt through in a small saucepan but do not boil.
8. Arrange the carrots on a large plate and pour over any of the oil left in the pan.
9. Pour the yogurt over the top, sprinkle with the mint, and serve immediately.

brass aghtsan

LEEKS WITH YOGURT SAUCE

A delightfully and delicately flavored accompaniment to fish or chicken dishes.

8 leeks

juice of 1 lemon

10 or more peppercorns

1 teaspoon salt

4 coriander seeds

3 sprigs of parsley

3 scallions, including green parts,
   finely chopped

2½ cups (½ l) yogurt mustard sauce
   (see p. 252)

2 tablespoons chopped parsley
   as a garnish

1. Cut off the roots and most of the green tops of the leeks and remove any coarse outer leaves.
2. Wash carefully under cold running water to remove all the grit and sand between the layers.
3. Prepare a stock; in a saucepan, bring 2 cups (½ l) of water to a boil. Add the lemon juice, peppercorns, salt, coriander seeds, parsley sprigs, and chopped onions, and simmer for about 10 minutes.
4. Arrange the leeks in a large frying pan or ovenproof dish and pour the stock over the top.
5. Cover and simmer gently for 20 to 30 minutes or until the leeks are tender.
6. Switch off the heat and leave to cool.
7. Remove the leeks and drain on paper towels.
8. Arrange the leeks on a large plate and pour the yogurt mustard sauce over the top.
9. Sprinkle with the chopped parsley and serve.

vospov tutum

LENTILS WITH PUMPKIN

Great recipes are often made with the simplest ingredients and nothing could be simpler than lentils or pumpkin. Serve with meat dishes, stews, and grills.

3 oz (75 g) whole brown lentils
1½ lb (¾ kg) peeled pumpkin
4 tablespoons (2 oz/50 g) butter
1 onion, finely chopped
1 oz (25 g) sugar

½ teaspoon salt
3 tablespoons finely chopped
  parsley
1¼ cups (300 ml) yogurt

1. Soak the lentils for a few hours in cold water and then rinse under cold running water.
2. Place the lentils in a saucepan and add sufficient water to cover by at least 1 in (about 3 cm).
3. Bring to a boil and simmer for about 30 minutes or until the lentils are tender, adding more water if necessary. Drain and set aside.
4. Meanwhile, cut the pumpkin flesh into slices 2 in (5 cm) long and ½ in (1 cm) thick.
5. Put the pumpkin pieces into a large saucepan and add enough water to cover by 1 in (about 3 cm).
6. Bring to a boil and simmer until the pumpkin is just tender. It will go mushy if overcooked.
7. Drain the pumpkin and set aside.
8. Melt the butter in a deep pan, add the onion, and sauté until it is golden brown.
9. Add the lentils and pumpkin, and sprinkle the sugar and salt over the top.
10. Mix them together gently, taking care not to break up the pumpkin.
11. Simmer for 3 to 5 minutes.
12. Pour the vegetables into a large serving dish and sprinkle with the parsley.
13. Serve with the yogurt on the side; 2–3 tablespoons stirred into each portion of vegetables will suffice.

borani ye gharch

YOGURT WITH MUSHROOMS

A Persian dish that can be eaten as an appetizer with salad and pita bread or as an accompaniment to any roast or grilled meat and to dumpling dishes.

1 lb (½ kg) mushrooms

4 tablespoons (2 oz/50 g) butter

1 cup (250 ml) chicken stock

2 cups (450 ml) yogurt

1 teaspoon salt

1 garlic clove, very finely chopped

1. Wash the mushrooms and pat dry on paper towels.
2. Slice the mushrooms.
3. Melt the butter in a saucepan and sauté the mushrooms for a few minutes.
4. Add the stock and simmer for 15 to 20 minutes until most of the liquid has evaporated.
5. Remove from the heat, drain the mushrooms, and leave to cool for a few minutes.
6. Add the yogurt and salt and stir well.
7. Sprinkle the garlic over the top.
8. Serve warm.

hungarian mushrooms in yogurt

This is a tasty mushroom dish that is an excellent accompaniment to any meat dish, either hot or cold.

¾ lb (350 g) mushrooms
4 tablespoons (2 oz/50 g) butter
1 onion, finely sliced
1 green pepper, finely sliced
1 tablespoon finely chopped parsley
¾ teaspoon salt

½ teaspoon black pepper
½ teaspoon paprika
generous ½ cup (150 ml) yogurt, stabilized with 1 tablespoon all-purpose flour (see p. 17)

1. Remove the stalks from the mushrooms, wipe the caps, and thinly slice.
2. Melt the butter in a large saucepan and fry the onion and green pepper until the onion slices are golden brown.
3. Add the mushrooms, 1 cup (200 ml) water, parsley, salt, black pepper, and paprika.
4. Stew the vegetables, stirring occasionally, until the water has evaporated.
5. Add the stabilized yogurt and heat through, but do not boil.
6. Serve immediately.

sautéed parsnips

A simple side dish that goes well with most roast meat and fish dishes.

2 lb (1 kg) parsnips
4 tablespoons (2 oz/50 g) butter
1 small onion, finely chopped
salt to taste

1¼ cups (300 ml) yogurt mustard
 sauce (see p. 252)
1 tablespoon chopped parsley

1. Cut the tops and roots off the parsnips, peel or scrape them, and wash.
2. Cut each one in half lengthwise and remove the hard core.
3. Half-fill a large saucepan with lightly-salted water, add the parsnips, and boil for 10 to 15 minutes or until just tender.
4. Drain and pat dry on paper towels.
5. Melt the butter in a large saucepan or frying pan, add the onion, and sauté for a few minutes.
6. Add the parsnips and fry gently for 5 minutes, turning occasionally. Season with salt to taste.
7. Arrange the vegetables on a large plate and pour the yogurt mustard sauce over the top.
8. Sprinkle with the chopped parsley and serve warm.

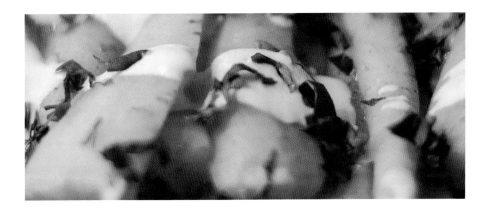

matar panir

PEAS WITH FRESH CHEESE

This is not strictly a yogurt dish, but I justify its inclusion on three grounds. First because it is made of *panir*—a fresh cheese, the recipe for which I have included on p. 19. Secondly, because it can also be made with *labna* (the Arab version of yogurt cheese, p. 18) or with *chortan* (the Armenian dried yogurt, p. 20). Add now the most important reason—because I like it.

If you possibly can, make your own *panir* or *labna* and trap the whey, as you need it for this recipe. If you prefer to buy the cheese try fresh Pecorino.

8 oz (250 g) *panir* or *labna*—made from 5 cups (1 l) yogurt—together with its whey (or use Pecorino mixed with a generous ½ cup/ 150 ml skim milk)	2 onions, finely sliced
	6 oz (175 g) fresh or frozen peas
	½ teaspoon paprika
	½ teaspoon ground ginger
	½ teaspoon *garam masala*
4 oz (125 g) ghee or butter	1 tablespoon finely chopped cilantro
½ teaspoon salt	or mint

1. Cut the cheese into ½ in (1 cm) cubes.
2. Melt the ghee or butter in a saucepan, add the cubes of cheese, and fry until they are a light brown.
3. In a bowl, mix the whey or skim milk with the salt.
4. Using a slotted spoon, remove the cheese cubes from the saucepan and place in the whey or milk to soak for about 15 minutes.
5. Meanwhile, fry the onions in the same ghee or butter until golden brown.
6. Remove the onions and set aside.
7. Put generous ½ cup (150 ml) water and the peas into the saucepan, bring to a boil, and simmer until the peas are just tender.
8. Drain the liquid, leaving the peas in the pan.
9. Return the onions and cheese to the pan together with the paprika and ginger and stir gently over a very low heat for 2 to 3 minutes.
10. Finally, add the *garam masala* and stir gently for a further 2 minutes.
11. Turn onto a serving dish, sprinkle with the cilantro or mint, and serve immediately.

yogurtlu patates

POTATOES WITH YOGURT AND CHIVES

A popular Balkan and Turkish specialty. The addition of whipped egg whites almost makes this a soufflé. It goes extremely well with all forms of roast meat.

2 lb (1 kg) potatoes, peeled, boiled in lightly-salted water, and drained
¼ cup yogurt
1 tablespoon butter
2 eggs, separated

1 tablespoon chopped chives
½ teaspoon dried thyme
¼ teaspoon paprika
salt and pepper to taste
a pinch of nutmeg

1. Preheat the oven to 350°F (180°C).
2. Mash the potatoes with the yogurt and butter until smooth.
3. Beat in the egg yolks, chives, thyme, paprika, salt, and pepper.
4. Lightly butter a soufflé dish.
5. Whisk the egg whites until stiff and gently fold into the potato mixture.
6. Spoon the mixture into the soufflé dish, smooth the surface, and sprinkle with nutmeg.
7. Bake for 25 to 30 minutes.
8. Serve immediately.

vegetable dishes

baigan pakorhas

EGGPLANT FRITTERS

Eggplants make excellent fritters. The batter will keep for weeks if covered and left in the refrigerator. This makes it very useful if you want hors d'oeuvre or afternoon snacks in a hurry. Bear in mind the following points:

1. Slice the eggplants ⅛ in (25mm) thick crosswise.
2. Make sure that the oil is not too hot or the fat and *pakorhas* will become a dirty brown, and not too cool or they will become laden with excess fat.

arshda madznov

ARMENIAN MACARONI MOUSSAKA

This dish can be an appetizer or a main course. It is an excellent vegetarian dish; it can also be served as an accompaniment to grilled or roast meat. You can use spaghetti instead of macaroni and you can also add either sliced mushrooms or sliced green peppers or both.

1 large or 2 medium eggplants
9 oz (250 g) cooked macaroni cut
   into 1 in (3 cm) pieces
2 or 3 tomatoes, thinly sliced
1¼ cups (300 ml) yogurt, stabilized
   with 1 tablespoon flour (see p. 17)

1¼ cups (300 ml) chicken stock
1 teaspoon salt
½ teaspoon black pepper
3 oz (75 g) grated cheese—
   Cheddar, Gruyère, or feta
1 oz (25 g) chopped almonds

1. Cut the stem and bottom from each eggplant, then wash and cut lengthwise into ¾ in (2 cm) pieces.
2. Preheat the oven to 350°F (180°C).
3. Put the macaroni in a well-buttered casserole.

4. Cover the macaroni first with the tomato slices and then layer on the eggplant slices.
5. Mix the yogurt and chicken stock together; season and spoon over the eggplants.
6. Mix the cheese and almonds together and sprinkle over the top of the casserole.
7. Bake for about an hour or until the top is golden brown.

patates me yaourti

STUFFED POTATOES

This is a simple, wholesome dish of Balkan origin. It makes a tasty lunch served with a fresh salad. If possible use feta cheese, otherwise any white cheese will do.

4 large potatoes
a little melted butter
2 oz (50 g) grated feta or
   white cheese
2 oz (50 g) cooked ground meat
   (lamb or beef)

2 tablespoons chopped chives
generous ½ cup (150 ml) yogurt
1 teaspoon salt
½ teaspoon black pepper
a pinch of nutmeg

1. Preheat the oven to 400°F (200°C) .
2. Wash and dry the potatoes.
3. Brush the potatoes with the melted butter and place in a lightly buttered ovenproof dish.
4. Bake for about 1 hour.
5. Remove from the oven and leave until cool enough to handle.
6. Remove a small slice from the top of each potato.
7. Using a small spoon, scoop out as much of the insides as possible and place in a mixing bowl. Take care not to break the potato shells.
7. Add the cheese, meat, chives, yogurt, salt, and pepper to the potato pieces and mix the ingredients together.

8. Fill each potato shell with the mixture.

9. Place any remaining filling in a small saucepan.

10. Rearrange the potatoes in the casserole, place a dab of butter on each, and bake for about 10 minutes.

11. Meanwhile, heat any remaining filling through, but be careful not to burn.

12. Place the extra filling in the middle of a large plate and arrange the potatoes around it.

13. Sprinkle with the nutmeg and serve immediately.

pancharegheni porani

ARMENIAN VEGETABLE STEW

This vegetarian dish can be eaten either as a main dish or as an accompaniment to roast meat. Serve with roast potatoes or a plain rice pilaf. It is a simple, wholesome, and economical dish.

3 medium eggplants
3 zucchinis
2 teaspoons salt
4 oz (100 g) green beans
8 tablespoons (4 oz/100 g) butter
1 green or red pepper, sliced

1 garlic clove, crushed
1 teaspoon black pepper
2 eggs
1¼ cups (300 ml) garlic yogurt sauce
  (see p. 247)
a pinch of paprika, to garnish

1. Remove the stems and tails of the eggplants and zucchinis.
2. Cut them into ¼ in (½ cm) slices.
3. Meanwhile, wash, top, and tail the green beans and cut into 2 in (5 cm) pieces.
4. Put the beans in a pan of boiling, lightly-salted water and cook for 5 to 10 minutes.
5. Drain and dry with paper towel.
6. Melt the butter in a large saucepan or casserole, add the eggplant and zucchini, and fry, stirring occasionally, for about 10 minutes.
7. Add the beans, green pepper, garlic, pepper, and 2 teaspoons salt.
8. Stir, cover, and simmer until all the vegetables are just cooked—about 20 minutes. Stir occasionally.
9. Break the eggs into a bowl, beat with a fork, and stir into the vegetables.
10. As soon as the egg is cooked remove from the heat.
11. Empty into a serving dish, spoon the garlic yogurt sauce over it, and sprinkle with the paprika.

gaghampi patoug

CABBAGE LEAVES STUFFED WITH MEAT

Stuffed cabbage—with or without meat—is popular in Turkey and Armenia. Armenians add garlic yogurt sauce to the stuffed leaves. Yogurt and bulgar have a great affinity for one another.

2–3 lb (1–1½ kg) white cabbage
1–2 teaspoons vinegar
4 oz (100 g) dried apricots
1 small onion, sliced
2 tablespoons tomato paste
stock or water
salt and pepper

4 oz (100 g) rice or coarse bulgar,
  washed thoroughly
1 teaspoon dried basil
1 teaspoon allspice
1 teaspoon black pepper
2 teaspoons salt
4 oz (100 g) chopped walnuts

FILLING
1 lb (½ kg) ground lamb
1 large onion, finely chopped
1 tablespoon chopped parsley

TO SERVE
2½ cups (½ l) garlic yogurt sauce
  (see p. 247)

1. Combine all the filling ingredients in a large bowl and knead well, adding about ½ cup (150 ml) cold water.
2. Cut the cabbage in half and gently separate the leaves.
3. Drop them into boiling water and cook gently for about 10 minutes until soft.
4. Drain and sprinkle with a little vinegar.
5. When cool, cut through the thickest part of the central vein so that the leaves lie flat, reserving any broken or damaged leaves.
6. Taking one leaf at a time, put a tablespoon of meat mixture in the center and wrap in the same way as *derevi patoug* (p. 141).
7. Line the base of a large saucepan with reserved broken leaves to prevent burning. Arrange the rolls in a tightly-packed layer and top with a layer of dried fruit and onion slices; repeat until all the rolls have been layered.
8. Dilute the tomato paste with enough stock or water to cover the rolls and season.
9. Cook for 1 hour or until the leaves are tender and the filling is cooked.
10. Serve immediately, accompanied by the garlic yogurt sauce.

yogurtlu biber dolmaci

GREEN PEPPERS STUFFED WITH MEAT AND YOGURT

This is an unusual variation of a dish popular throughout the Middle East.
The peppers in this recipe are stuffed with meat, nuts, breadcrumbs, and yogurt.
Serve them hot with rice and salad as a main meal or warm as an appetizer.

4 large green peppers
4 tablespoons (2 oz/50 g) ghee or
  butter
1 onion, finely chopped
1 oz (25 g) mushrooms, thinly sliced
8 oz (225 g) ground meat—lamb is
  the traditional choice, but beef is
  perfectly acceptable

1 teaspoon salt
½ teaspoon black pepper
1 oz (25 g) breadcrumbs
1 tablespoon chopped parsley
2 tablespoons pine nuts—if
  unavailable use coarsely
  chopped walnuts
1 cup (250 ml) yogurt

1. Cut a thin slice from the stalk end of each pepper. Retain the stalks.
2. Remove the seeds and white pith.
3. Melt the ghee or butter in a saucepan and sauté the onion and mushrooms
   until soft.
4. Add the meat and cook for about 15 minutes, stirring frequently.
5. Season with the salt and pepper and remove from the heat.
6. In a large bowl, combine the breadcrumbs, parsley, pine nuts or walnuts, the
   meat mixture, and the yogurt and mix well.
7. Preheat the oven to 375°F (190°C).
8. Fill the peppers with this mixture. Press the filling down tightly and replace
   the tops.
9. Standing the peppers upright, fit them tightly into an ovenproof dish.
10. Add about 1 in (3 cm) water and bake for 30 to 40 minutes.

sheikh-el-mahshi bi laban

STUFFED ZUCCHINI IN YOGURT SAUCE

This is one of the most popular dishes from Aleppo, Syria, which is famed for its rich and spicy cuisine. A good accompaniment is a rice pilaf.

2 tablespoons (25 g) ghee or unsalted butter, the best substitute for the *hamma* used in Syria

1 onion, finely chopped

1 lb (½ kg) ground lamb or beef

1½ teaspoons salt

½ teaspoon black pepper

1 teaspoon allspice

2 oz (50 g) pine nuts—if unavailable use coarsely chopped walnuts

12 medium-sized zucchinis

2½ cups (½ l) yogurt, stabilized with 2 eggs (see p. 17)

2 tablespoons (1 oz/25 g) butter

1 garlic clove, crushed

1 teaspoon dried mint

1. Heat the ghee or butter in a large frying pan, add the onion, and sauté until soft and transparent.
2. Add the meat and fry, stirring frequently, over a fairly high heat until the meat is dark brown.
3. Lower the heat and stir in the salt, pepper, allspice, and pine nuts.
4. Add a few tablespoons of water, cover, and simmer for at least 30 minutes or until the meat is very tender.
5. Meanwhile, prepare the zucchinis by first slicing off the stalk ends.
6. Remove as much of the flesh as possible with an apple corer. Ideally the vegetable shell should be about ¼ in (½ cm) thick. Take care not to split or make holes in the shells.
7. Fill each zucchini with the meat mixture.
8. Arrange the zucchinis in a large saucepan and place a plate over the top to hold them in place.
9. Add sufficient lightly-salted water to cover, bring to a boil, and then lower the heat and simmer until the vegetables are tender.
10. Pour the stabilized yogurt into a small bowl and stir in a few tablespoons of the hot stock.

11. Remove saucepan from the heat, and remove the plate.
12. Slowly add the yogurt to the pan, place back on the stovetop, and simmer over very low heat.
13. Melt the butter in a small pan, add the garlic and mint, fry for a few minutes, and pour into the saucepan.
14. Taste and season with a little more salt if necessary.
15. Serve immediately.

derevi patoug
STUFFED VINE LEAVES

Stuffed vegetables and fruit are a traditional part of Middle Eastern cuisine. Whereas Arabs, Turks, and Greeks use rice, Armenians prefer to use bulgar, and usually serve a yogurt sauce with the vegetables. In this version the leaves are wrapped around a filling of meat and spices. If a vine is available then pick the leaves in late May or early June when they are at their tenderest.

1 lb (½ kg) vine leaves, fresh
　or preserved

2 teaspoons salt
1 teaspoon black pepper
1 teaspoon allspice

FILLING
1 lb (½ kg) ground lamb
1 onion, finely chopped
1 green pepper, chopped
2 tablespoons chopped parsley
6 oz (175 g) coarse bulgar
2 tomatoes, blanched, skinned, and
　chopped
2 tablespoons chopped fresh
　herbs e.g. cilantro, mint, basil,
　marjoram
2 oz (50 g) pine nuts or roughly
　chopped walnuts

SAUCE
sufficient stock or water to
　cover the leaves
2 tablespoons tomato paste
2 garlic cloves, crushed
juice of 1 lemon
salt and pepper to taste

TO SERVE
2½ cups (600 ml) garlic yogurt
　sauce (see p. 247)

1. If you are using fresh vine leaves, pick young and tender ones. If using preserved ones kept in brine, rinse under cold running water first.
2. Fill a sacuepan with salted water and bring to a boil. Immerse the fresh leaves in the water and boil for 2 to 3 minutes. Pour off the water and spread out the leaves on paper towels to dry.
3. In a large bowl, combine all the filling ingredients and knead until the mixture is well blended and smooth.
4. To fill the vine leaves: first lay one leaf out flat, smooth side down and veins facing up.
5. Cut off the stalk. Arrange a small ridge of filling across the center at the widest part of the leaf. Fold the bottom of the leaf up over the filling. Fold the sides over towards the center. Roll up towards the tip to the leaf.
6. You will now have a small cigar-shaped parcel.
7. Repeat until the leaves and filling are used up, reserving any damaged leaves.
8. Use any remaining broken leaves to line the bottom of a medium to large saucepan—this helps to prevent burning.
9. Pack the stuffed vine leaves carefully and tightly in layers.
10. Place a large plate, bottom side up, over the leaves, covering as many as possible, and hold it down with a small weight. This will prevent the leaves moving around while cooking and coming undone.
11. Mix all the sauce ingredients together and pour into the saucepan.
12. Bring to a boil and then simmer for about 1 hour or until the stuffing is cooked and the leaves tender. It may be necessary to add a little more water.
13. Arrange the vine leaves on a large platter and serve with the garlic yogurt sauce. It is normally poured over the stuffed leaves.
14. Reserve any remaining stock and use it to reheat any stuffed leaves not consumed immediately.

pakorhas

VEGETABLE AND YOGURT FRITTERS

Pakorhas are traditionally vegetable savories but you can use fruit as well. The most popular *pakorhas* are *baigan pakorha* (eggplant), *saag pakorha* (spinach), and *praza pakorha* (onion). They are often found on the menus of good Indian restaurants.

The art of successful *pakorhas* is in the batter, which is made with *besan—* chickpea flour—obtainable from most Indian stores and natural food stores. The recipe below is for *praza pakorhas—*onion *pakorhas.*

½ teaspoon chili powder

½ teaspoon turmeric

1 teaspoon salt

1 teaspoon *garam masala*

6 oz (175 g) *besan* (chickpea flour)

2½ cups (600 ml) yogurt

1 garlic clove, crushed

2 onions

⅔-1¼ cups (150–300 ml)
   vegetable oil for frying

1. Sieve the chili powder, turmeric, salt, *garam masala*, and *besan* into a bowl.
2. In a large bowl, combine the yogurt and garlic and whisk until smooth.
3. Sifting the dry mixture again, add it a little at a time to the yogurt, stirring continuously, preferably with a wire whisk.
4. Keep whisking until you have a smooth batter that forms small peaks that disintegrate after 15 to 20 seconds. You may find that you need a little more or less flour depending on how liquid the yogurt is.
5. Leave the batter to stand for 30 minutes and then whisk once more.
6. Meanwhile, peel the onions and slice crosswise to form onion rings.
7. Heat the oil in a large pan.
8. Dip each onion ring into the batter and fry individually in the vegetable oil until pale golden on both sides.
9. Lift out with a slotted spoon and drain on paper towels.
10. Repeat with the remaining rings.
11. If you like the *pakorhas* very crisp, then return them to the hot oil for about 20 seconds just before serving. Drain and serve immediately.

egg dishes

egg dishes

tzvadzegh

OMELET

Yogurt can be used extensively as an accompaniment to all kinds of omelets. Serve it plain, with garlic, or with herbs. I have chosen a few recipes to show the possibilities. Experiment to your heart's content.

SERVES ONE

2 eggs
¼ teaspoon paprika
salt to taste
2 tablespoons (1 oz/25 g) butter

1 teaspoon chopped parsley
generous ½ cup (150 g) plain yogurt
or garlic yogurt sauce (see p. 247)

1. Break the eggs into a small bowl, add the paprika and salt, and whisk with a fork.
2. Melt the butter in a small frying pan.
3. Pour the egg mixture into the pan, stir with the fork, and cook over a medium heat.
4. When the omelet is just set, sprinkle the parsley over the top, fold in half, and slide on to a plate.
5. Serve either with plain yogurt or garlic yogurt sauce.

basturma or yershig omelet

Two of my favorite omelets require ingredients which are, unfortunately, rather difficult to track down. You may find them in Greek, Armenian, or Middle Eastern stores. They are: *basturma*—raw dried beef which is salted, covered with a mixture of spices, including fenugreek, and then hung up to dry in a cool place for days; and *yershig*—meat sausage highly spiced with garlic, chili, and other spices. If you cannot find this then you could use a garlic-seasoned sausage instead.

1. Fry the *basturma* or *yershig* in the butter and then proceed as with the plain omelet (see p. 145).

bargoog chor tzvadzegh

APRICOT OMELET

3 dried apricots, quartered

A recipe from the Erzenjan, eastern Turkey.

1. Fry the apricots for a few minutes in butter, then proceed as for the plain omelet (see p. 145).

enguizi missov tzvadzegh

OMELET WITH MEAT AND WALNUTS

This is a typical Armenian omelet, especially popular in the winter months. It is often eaten as a snack with *lavash* or pita bread. However, with fried potatoes and a bowl of salad it makes an inexpensive main meal.

4 tablespoons (2 oz/50 g) ghee
  or butter
1 lb (½ kg) ground beef or lamb
1 onion, finely chopped
4 oz (100 g) walnuts, coarsely
  chopped
1 teaspoon salt
½ teaspoon black pepper

½ teaspoon ground cumin
8 eggs
1¼ cups (300 ml) garlic yogurt sauce
  (see p. 247)
1 teaspoon paprika
tomato slices, radishes, and
  scallions, to garnish

1. Melt the ghee or butter in a large frying pan, add the ground meat, and fry, stirring frequently, until the meat is lightly browned.
2. Add the chopped onion and fry for a few more minutes.
3. Now add the walnuts, salt, black pepper, and cumin, and fry for 15 to 20 minutes, stirring frequently.
4. Break the eggs into a bowl and beat with a fork.
5. Pour the eggs into the pan and fry gently until the eggs are set.
6. Slide the omelet on to a plate, pour the garlic yogurt sauce over the top, sprinkle with the paprika, and serve at once with the garnishes.

pasha's omelet

This is my adaptation of a Turkish omelet. I have added mushrooms and tomatoes to give it extra flavor and color.

2 tablespoons (1 oz/25 g) butter
1 onion, finely chopped
6 button mushrooms, wiped clean
  and thinly sliced
2 tomatoes, finely chopped
8 eggs

3 tablespoons grated Parmesan
  cheese
generous ½ cup (150 ml) yogurt
1 garlic clove, crushed
½ teaspoon cumin
½ teaspoon paprika

1. Preheat to 400°F (200°C).
2. In a shallow ovenproof dish, melt the butter over a moderate heat and sauté the onion until soft.
3. Add the mushrooms and tomatoes and cook until soft.
4. Beat the eggs and pour over the vegetables.
5. Sprinkle the Parmesan cheese over the top.
6. Place in the oven and cook until set and light gold.
7. Meanwhile, beat the yogurt and garlic together in a small saucepan and heat through but do not boil.
8. Remove the egg dish from the oven, pour the yogurt over the eggs, and sprinkle with the cumin and paprika.
9. Serve immediately.

dzedzadz missov tzvadzegh

GROUND MEAT WITH EGGS AND YOGURT

Serve this dish with a bowl of fresh salad and pickles.

4 tablespoons (2 oz/50 g) butter	½ teaspoon black pepper
1 onion, finely chopped	2 tablespoons chopped parsley
1 garlic clove, crushed	4 eggs
½ lb (225 g) ground lamb or beef	2 teaspoons paprika
2 tablespoons tomato paste	1¼ cups (300 ml) yogurt
½ teaspoon allspice	
1 teaspoon salt	

1. Melt half the butter in a frying pan and sauté the onion and garlic until soft.
2. Add the meat and cook well, stirring frequently.
3. Add the tomato paste, allspice, salt, and pepper, and stir well.
4. Add a generous ½ cup (150 ml) water and cook slowly for a further 15 minutes.
5. Stir in the parsley.

6. Make four depressions in the mixture with the back of a tablespoon.
7. Break an egg into each depression.
8. Meanwhile, melt the remaining butter and add the paprika.
9. Mix this with the yogurt and then pour it over the eggs.
10. Cook slowly until the eggs have set. Serve immediately.

anda-dahi kari

EGG CURRY WITH YOGURT

This is a simple but delightful dish from the Indian subcontinent. It is cheap to make and played a major part in the diet of my student days. Eat with a plain rice pilaf or *chapatis* and chutney.

3 tablespoons (1½ oz/40 g) ghee
  or butter
1 onion, finely chopped
2 teaspoons turmeric
½ teaspoon chili powder
½ teaspoon ground ginger
1 tablespoon *garam masala*

1 teaspoon salt
½ teaspoon black pepper
1 teaspoon lemon juice
1¼ cups (300 ml) yogurt, stabilized
  (see p. 17)
8 hard-boiled eggs

1. Melt the ghee or butter in a large saucepan and sauté the onion until soft.
2. Add the turmeric, chili powder, ginger, *garam masala*, salt, and pepper.
3. Cook very gently, stirring frequently, for about 20 to 30 minutes.
4. Add the lemon juice and yogurt; stir, and heat through.
5. Shell the eggs, cut into quarters, and add to the mixture.
6. Stir very gently and simmer for a further 15 minutes.
7. Serve immediately.

eggeh mughrabi

MOROCCAN SCRAMBLED EGGS

This is a well-loved North African egg dish normally prepared without yogurt, but I have found yogurt combines very well with the vegetables, enhancing them with its unique flavor.

4 tablespoons (2 oz/50 g) ghee
  or butter
1 onion, sliced
1 garlic clove, crushed
2 tomatoes, sliced
1 green pepper, seeded and
  thinly sliced

½ teaspoon oregano
½ teaspoon chili powder
1 teaspoon salt
¼ teaspoon black pepper
4 eggs
2 tablespoons chopped parsley
1¼ cups (150 ml) yogurt

1. Melt the ghee or butter in a large frying pan, add the onion and garlic, and sauté until soft.
2. Add the tomatoes, green pepper, oregano, chili powder, salt, and black pepper, and cook for 10 to 15 minutes or until the vegetables are tender.
3. Place the eggs, parsley, and yogurt in a bowl and whisk.
4. Pour this mixture into the pan and cook over a low heat, stirring frequently, until set.
5. Serve immediately, with salad and bread.

saray yumurtasi

EGG AND TOMATO, PALACE STYLE

This is an adaptation of a Turkish egg dish. It makes an excellent appetizer and looks splendid as part of a cold buffet.

4 large tomatoes
8 eggs
2 chicken breasts, cooked and
　finely chopped
2 cornichons, finely sliced
24 black olives

1¼ cups (300 ml) garlic yogurt
　sauce (p. 247) or Orga's
　yogurt dressing (p. 245)
1 teaspoon paprika
2 tablespoons chopped parsley

1. Cut the tomatoes in half; spoon out the pulp and discard.
2. Poach the eggs in water until just firm.
3. Using a slotted spoon, place one egg into the cavity of each tomato half.
4. Arrange the tomatoes around a large plate leaving the center empty.
5. Heap the chicken into the center.
6. Chill for 1 hour.
7. Arrange the sliced cornichons and the black olives decoratively around the tomatoes.
8. Pour the yogurt dressing over and garnish with the paprika and parsley.
9. Serve immediately.

cilbir

EGG ON TOAST WITH SPICED YOGURT

This is a traditional Turkish recipe that makes an excellent savory snack. The eggs are usually fried, but you can poach them if you wish.

SERVES SIX

5 tablespoons (2½ oz/65 g) butter	1 level teaspoon salt
6 eggs	½ teaspoon black pepper
6 large slices of toast	½ teaspoon cumin
6 slices cooked tongue (optional)	1 teaspoon paprika
1¼ cups (300 ml) yogurt	

1. Melt 3 tablespoons (1½ oz/40 g) butter in a large frying pan and break the eggs gently into the pan.
2. Cook until just firm.
3. Meanwhile, arrange the toast on a large platter and place a slice of tongue on top of each.
4. Place 1 egg on top of each slice of toast.
5. Beat the yogurt with the salt, pepper, and cumin until creamy.
6. Pour a little of this mixture over each egg.
7. Melt the remaining 2 tablespoons (1 oz/25 g) butter, mix with the paprika, and spoon over the eggs.
8. Serve immediately.

eggs en cocotte

Here is a yogurt version of the French classic.

2 rashers Canadian bacon, rind and bone removed, diced	salt and pepper to taste
4 eggs	2 oz (50 g) grated Parmesan cheese
8 tablespoons yogurt	2 tablespoons chopped parsley

1. Preheat the oven to 350°F (180°C).
2. Divide the bacon between four ramekins or individual soufflé dishes.
3. Bake on the top shelf of the oven for 10 minutes.
4. Break an egg into each dish.
5. Add 2 tablespoons of yogurt to each dish (do not let the yogurt cover the yolks).

6. Season with the salt and pepper.
7. Sprinkle the cheese over the yogurt (make sure the yogurt is covered).
8. Bake for 10 minutes on the top shelf of the oven, until the eggs are lightly set.
9. Serve in the dishes, garnished with chopped parsley.

macedonian poached eggs

This is a Balkan specialty that is also found throughout the Middle East. It makes use of spinach, which goes extremely well with yogurt and eggs. It makes a fine hors d'oeuvre or snack.

1 lb (½ kg) frozen spinach
salt
a little butter
8 eggs
2 garlic cloves, crushed

1¼ cups (300 ml) yogurt
4 oz (100 g) grated Parmesan cheese
2 tablespoons finely chopped
　parsley

1. Thaw spinach.
2. Place in a pan of boiling salted water and simmer for 8 to 10 minutes.
3. Drain in a colander and, when cool enough to handle, squeeze out any excess water.
4. Place the spinach on a wooden board and chop.
5. Lightly butter a large shallow baking dish. Preheat the oven to 300°F (150°C).
6. Arrange the spinach in a layer over the base of the dish.
7. With the back of a spoon make eight depressions in the spinach.
8. Break an egg into each depression.
9. In a small bowl, mix together the garlic, yogurt, and cheese, and spoon some of the mixture over each egg, making sure the mixture doesn't cover the yolks.
10. Sprinkle the parsley over the eggs.
11. Bake until the eggs are just set and are bubbly and golden on top.
12. Serve immediately—one egg per person if you are serving this dish as an hors d'oeuvre or two per person if it is to be served as a lunch.

meat dishes

In the Middle East, parts of the Balkans, and the north Indian subcontinent, yogurt is not only consumed on its own or with other ingredients as part of a meal in soups and salads, but it is often cooked with meats. Lamb or mutton are still the most popular meats throughout these regions, while pork, outside the Christian lands, is completely ignored since both the Islamic and Jewish faiths forbid it. Yogurt is also used as a side dish for roast meats, kebabs, and pilafs. Indeed, to many Turks and Iranians, the greatest and tastiest meal in the world is a bowl of rice pilaf accompanied by a bowl of plain yogurt, bread, and fresh vegetables, such as cucumbers, onions, tomatoes, and radishes. Hence the Iranian expression: A bowl of *chelo, mast,* and greens to me; the keys of Paradise to thee.

kebabcheh

MEATBALLS WITH RICE IN YOGURT SAUCE

This Ottoman-style recipe from Bulgaria is distantly related to a dish known as *Ismir kufta,* which is made with tomatoes. It is not a true kebab as it is cooked in a saucepan. Serve with plain rice pilaf and a fresh salad.

1 lb (½ kg) ground meat
1 small onion, finely chopped
1 egg
¼ cup fresh breadcrumbs
1½ teaspoons salt
1 heaped teaspoon dried marjoram

or 1 tablespoon chopped
fresh marjoram
2½ cups (600 ml) beef stock
2 tablespoons rice, washed
generous ½ cup (150 ml) yogurt
2 egg yolks

1. In a bowl, combine the meat, onion, egg, breadcrumbs, salt, and marjoram.
2. Knead until the mixture is smooth.
3. Divide the mixture into twenty small lumps and, with damp palms, roll them into small balls.

4. Pour the stock into a large saucepan and bring it to a boil.
5. Carefully spoon the meatballs into the pan, cover, and simmer for 15 minutes.
6. Very carefully, stir in the rice and simmer for a further 20 minutes.
7. Carefully lift the meatballs from the stock, place in a heatproof dish, and keep warm.
8. In a small bowl, beat the egg yolks into the yogurt.
9. Turn the heat to very low and gradually stir the yogurt mixture into the rice and stock.
10. Stir continuously until the sauce thickens, but do not let it boil.
11. Pour the sauce over the meatballs and serve immediately.

kofta kari

CURRIED MEATBALLS IN YOGURT

This is one of the most popular and inexpensive of all Indian curry dishes. It is a must for all festive occasions.

1 lb (½ kg) ground meat

2 onions

4 garlic cloves, peeled

a handful of parsley, stalks removed

1 egg

2 teaspoons salt

vegetable oil for frying

4 tablespoons (2 oz/50 g) ghee or butter

2 teaspoons chili powder

1 teaspoon black pepper

1 teaspoon ground cumin

1 tablespoon *garam masala*

1 tablespoon paprika

1 teaspoon turmeric

½ oz (15 g) chopped fresh ginger

2 cups (450 ml) yogurt

1. Pass the ground meat through a meat grinder together with one of the onions, (roughly chopped), 2 garlic cloves, and the parsley (or use in a food processor).
2. Place this mixture in a bowl; add the egg and 1 teaspoon salt and knead until smooth.

3. With damp hands, shape the meat into small walnut-sized balls.

4. Heat some oil in a large frying pan and fry the balls for 2 to 3 minutes, turning and browning on all sides.

5. Meanwhile, thinly slice the other onion and finely chop the remaining 2 garlic cloves. In a large saucepan, melt the ghee or butter and fry the onion and garlic until golden brown.

6. Add a teaspoon of salt and the spices and cook over a low heat for about 10 minutes, stirring frequently.

7. Add the meatballs, cover, and simmer over a low heat for 20 to 30 minutes, turning them frequently.

8. Remove from the heat and slowly stir in the yogurt.

9. Simmer gently for a further 30 to 40 minutes.

10. Serve on a bed of rice pilaf.

bosanske cufte

BOSNIAN-STYLE MEATBALLS

This is a Bosnian favorite of Ottoman origin. *Kufta* means ground meat in Arabic and it has passed into the Turkish language. This dish is distantly related to *Ismir kufta* and the Bulgarian *Kebabcheh*. Traditional accompaniments are a rice pilaf and green salad.

1 lb (½ kg) ground lamb or beef
2 oz (50 g) flour
1 egg
1 tablespoon finely chopped parsley
salt and pepper to taste

SAUCE
1¼ cups (300 ml) yogurt
2 eggs
1 teaspoon caraway seeds, crushed
salt and pepper to taste
½ teaspoon ground cumin

1. Preheat the oven to 350°F (180°C).

2. In a large bowl, combine the meat, flour, egg, parsley, salt, and pepper and knead until the mixture is smooth.

3. Keeping the palms of your hands damp, form the mixture into small balls, slightly smaller than a walnut.
4. Grease a shallow baking dish or casserole and arrange the meatballs in it.
5. Bake for 45 minutes.
6. Prepare the sauce by mixing together all the ingredients.
7. Remove the baking dish from the oven and transfer the meatballs to another shallow ovenproof dish.
8. Pour the sauce over the meatballs and return to the oven for a further 20 to 30 minutes until the mixture is set and golden brown.

borani-ye bademjan goosht

MEATBALLS WITH EGGPLANT IN YOGURT AND SAFFRON SAUCE

This was a favorite of Queen Pourandokht of Persia. It is particularly popular in the Azerbaijan region of Iran and is similar to the *kufte* (meatballs) of the Balkan, Arab, Turkish, and Armenian cuisines. Serve with rice pilaf.

1 large eggplant
2 onions
1 lb (½ kg) ground beef
1 teaspoon salt
½ teaspoon black pepper
4 tablespoons (2 oz/50 g) butter
generous ½ cup (150 ml) stock
   or water

1 tablespoon lemon juice
½ teaspoon ground saffron
2 cups (450 ml) yogurt, stabilized
   with 2 tablespoons flour (see p. 17)
1 tablespoon dried mint
a little melted butter

1. Remove head and tail of the eggplant and peel it.
2. Quarter it lengthwise and then cut crosswise into ¼ in (½ cm) slices.
3. If desired, spread the slices on a large plate, sprinkle with salt, and leave for ½ hour. Rinse them under cold water and pat dry with paper towels.
4. Finely chop 1 onion and place in a large mixing bowl with the meat, salt, and pepper.

6. Knead the mixture until smooth and then, with damp palms, shape it into small meatballs.

7. Preheat the oven to 350°F (180°C).

8. Thinly slice the remaining onion.

9. Melt 2 tablespoons (1 oz/25 g) butter in a large saucepan and sauté the sliced onion until it is golden brown.

10. Add the meatballs and sauté until browned all over, stirring frequently.

11. Add the stock and lemon juice, lower the heat, and simmer for about 5 to 10 minutes, stirring occasionally.

12. Meanwhile, melt the remaining 2 tablespoons (1 oz/25 g) butter in a large frying pan and sauté the sliced eggplant until brown on both sides. Add more butter if necessary.

13. Lightly butter a large ovenproof baking dish, arrange the meatballs and onion in the bottom, and place the eggplant slices over the top.

14. Mix the saffron into the stabilized yogurt and pour over the meat and eggplant.

15. Place in the oven and bake for 20 to 30 minutes.

16. When ready to serve, sauté the mint in a little melted butter for a few minutes, pour over the dish, and serve immediately.

keema seekh kebab

GROUND MEAT ON SKEWERS

This is a north Indian recipe for kebabs. Kebabs, of course, arrived in that subcontinent via the Middle East and Persia, but the ginger, *garam masala*, and chickpea flour give this recipe an authentic Indian flavor.

1 lb (½ kg) ground lamb or beef

2 tablespoons *besan* (chickpea flour)

1 onion, finely chopped

2 tablespoons finely chopped
 fresh cilantro

1 garlic clove, crushed

1 teaspoon finely grated
 fresh ginger

1 teaspoon salt

1 teaspoon *garam masala*

¼ cup (75 ml) yogurt

1. Combine the ground meat with all the other ingredients except the yogurt.
2. Knead until the mixture becomes very smooth.
3. Form small handfuls of the mixture into sausage shapes around flat skewers.
4. Beat the yogurt and coat the meat with it, then place the kebabs over a hot grill for 10 to 15 minutes, turning frequently. If you do not have a grill, you can place the kebabs under a broiler instead.
5. Serve with rice or Indian bread.

lamb tikka kebab

This dish, now a classic of the Indian subcontinent, was introduced by the invading Muslims from Arabia and Persia and then "Indianized" with time. Prepare two days in advance.

2 lb (1 kg) lean lamb, cut into
   1 in (3 cm) cubes

MARINADE
1¼ cups (300 ml) yogurt
1½ teaspoons *garam masala*

½ teaspoon ground coriander
½ teaspoon turmeric
2 garlic cloves, crushed
¼ teaspoon ground nutmeg
¾ teaspoon chili pepper
2 teaspoons ground cumin
grated rind and juice of 2 lemons

1. Mix all the marinade ingredients together in a large bowl.
2. Add the cubed meat, mix well, cover, and leave to marinate in the refrigerator for 2 days, stirring occasionally.
3. Thread on to skewers and grill until cooked through—about 15 to 20 minutes.
4. Serve garnished with onion rings and lemon wedges.
5. Eat with bread, e.g. *paratha*, *lavash*, or pita.

kabab halabi

ALEPPO KEBAB WITH YOGURT

A classic of Middle Eastern cuisine, this dish is also known as *madznov kebab* among the Armenians and *yogurtlu kebab* by the Turks. It originated in the region of Aleppo in northern Syria where some of the most exciting Middle Eastern dishes come from.

2 lb (1 kg) lean lamb, cut into
   1 in (3 cm) cubes
2 tablespoons olive oil
juice of 1 onion (or 1 very finely
   minced onion)
3 pita breads

4 tablespoons (2 oz/50 g) ghee
   or butter, melted
3 large tomatoes
½ teaspoon salt
2 cups (450 ml) yogurt
6 scallions, finely chopped
1 tablespoon finely chopped parsley

1. Put the meat into a large bowl, add the oil and onion juice or minced onion, mix well, and leave to marinate for 2 hours at room temperature.
2. Just before you cook the kebabs, warm the pitas over the grill or in the oven and then cut them into ½ in (1 cm) wide strips and place on a large serving platter.
3. Pour the melted butter over the bread, mix well, arrange the pieces neatly, and set aside to keep warm.
4. Thread the pieces of meat on skewers and grill for about 15 minutes, turning frequently.
5. Meanwhile, peel and chop the tomatoes.
6. Put the chopped tomatoes into a small frying pan and cook gently for about 3 minutes.
7. Season the tomatoes with the salt.
8. Once the kebabs are cooked, pour the tomatoes over the bread and then slide the meat off the skewers onto the tomatoes.
9. Pour the yogurt over the meat.
10. Sprinkle the chopped onion and parsley over the top and serve immediately.

khozi tap-tap

GROUND PORK AND BULGAR KEBAB

This dish comes from Sis, the capital of Cilician Armenia.

8 oz (250 g) fine bulgar	salt and pepper to taste
1 lb (½ kg) lean ground pork	2 oz (50 g) sesame seeds
1 onion, very finely chopped	1¼ cups (300 ml) yogurt
2 teaspoons cumin	½ teaspoon chili powder
1 teaspoon oregano	1 garlic clove, finely chopped

1. Soak the bulgar in cold water for 10 minutes, then drain in a fine sieve.
2. In a large bowl, combine the bulgar, meat, onion, cumin, oregano, salt, and pepper.
3. Knead the mixture for about 10 minutes, occasionally dampening your hands with cold water.
4. Divide the mixture into four portions and, using your hands, mold each one into a patty about 6 in (15 cm) in diameter and ½ in (1 cm) thick.
5. Before cooking, sprinkle some sesame seeds on both sides of the kebabs.
6. Cook on the grill or under the broiler, turning frequently to prevent burning. This should take about 10 minutes.
7. When cooked, serve on a plate topped with a mixture of fresh yogurt, chili powder, and garlic.
8. Serve with a plate of fresh salad or pickles.

amram

GROUND LAMB AND BULGAR KEBAB

Another favorite from Sis makes use of ground leg of lamb (or beef). Follow the recipe above, but omit oregano and sesame seeds, and substitute lamb for pork.

veal in yogurt kebab

This light and extremely tasty veal kebab is marinated in yogurt.

1 cup (200 ml) yogurt
1 garlic clove, crushed
1 large onion, finely chopped
salt and pepper to taste
1 lb (½ kg) shoulder of veal,
   cut into 1 in (3 cm) cubes

2 onions, quartered
3 tomatoes, halved
1 green pepper, white pith and
   seeds removed, cut into 8 pieces
1 teaspoon paprika

1. Mix the yogurt, garlic, chopped onion, salt, and pepper together in a large bowl.
2. Add the meat, mix well, cover, and leave to marinate for 4 to 6 hours.
3. Thread the meat on to skewers, alternating the pieces of meat with the onion quarters, tomato halves, and pepper pieces.
4. Cook on the grill or under the broiler for 15 to 20 minutes. If the meat looks as though it is drying, brush with a little olive oil.
5. Slide the kebabs onto a plate and sprinkle with the paprika.
6. Heat up the remaining marinade, but do not boil, and serve as an accompanying sauce.

czango goulash

GYPSY-STYLE GOULASH

Needless to say this is a Hungarian specialty, with a difference, in that it does not contain all the ingredients traditionally associated with goulash: onions, paprika, potatoes, and pasta. *Czango* has sauerkraut, rice, and caraway seeds, which give it its distinctive flavor. I have substituted yogurt for the traditional sour cream.

4 tablespoons (2 oz/50 g) lard
   or butter
1 onion, thinly sliced
1 garlic clove, crushed
1 tablespoon paprika
1 tablespoon caraway seeds
2 lb (1 kg) sirloin steak, cut into
   2 in (5 cm) pieces

2 teaspoons salt
1 lb (½ kg) sauerkraut
2 green peppers, seeded and sliced
3 oz (75 g) rice, washed thoroughly
2½ cups (600 ml) yogurt, stabilized
   with 1 egg or 1 tablespoon all-
   purpose flour (see p. 17)

1. Melt the lard or butter in a large saucepan and fry the onion and garlic until golden brown.
2. Add the paprika, caraway seeds, 1¼ cups (300 ml) water, steak, and salt, stir, cover, and allow to simmer gently for about 1½ hours.
3. Wash the sauerkraut under cold running water and add to the pan together with the sliced green peppers.
4. Add sufficient water to cover and continue cooking until the meat is tender.
5. Add the rice, stir, and cook for a further 10 to 12 minutes.
6. Just before serving, fold in the yogurt and heat through but do not boil.
7. Serve immediately.

yogurt moussaka

Here is a variation of the traditional moussaka found on the menu of any self-respecting Greek restaurant.

4 tablespoons (2 oz/50 g) butter
1 garlic clove, crushed
1 onion, finely chopped
2 large eggplants
1 lb (½ kg) tomatoes, fresh or
   canned, roughly chopped; include
   the juice if using canned ones
1 teaspoon dried oregano or 1
   tablespoon fresh oregano

¾ lb (350 g) ground lamb or beef
½ teaspoon dried rosemary or
   ½ tablespoon fresh rosemary
1 teaspoon salt
½ teaspoon black pepper
1¼ cups (300 ml) yogurt
1 egg yolk
1 tablespoon Parmesan cheese,
   grated

1. Melt the butter in a large ovenproof casserole.
2. Add the garlic and onion and sauté until soft and transparent.
3. Cut the heads and tails off the eggplants and cut lengthwise into ¼ in (½ cm) slices.
4. Add the eggplant slices to the casserole and cook for about 10 minutes, stirring frequently. Add a little more butter if necessary.
5. Add the tomatoes, meat, oregano, rosemary, salt, and pepper.
6. Cover and simmer for 30 to 45 minutes or until the meat is cooked.
7. Preheat the oven to 350°F (180°C).
7. Place the yogurt and egg yolk in a small pan and beat vigorously.
8. Cook over a low heat for about 10 minutes, stirring continuously.
9. Pour the yogurt sauce over the meat and vegetables and sprinkle the cheese over the top.
10. Place in the oven and bake for about 30 minutes.
11. Serve immediately.

marjoram tokány

MARJORAM STEW

A really delicious stew from Hungary that gains its distinctive flavor from the addition of marjoram.

2 lb (1 kg) beef steak, fillet, sirloin, or rump

2 oz (50 g) lard

2 onions, finely chopped

2 tablespoons chopped fresh marjoram or 1 tablespoon dried marjoram

1 teaspoon salt

½ teaspoon black pepper

1¼ cups (300 ml) dry white wine

8 oz (250 g) smoked Canadian bacon, rind and bones removed

1 garlic clove, crushed

2½ cups (600 ml) yogurt, stabilized with 1 egg or 1 tablespoon all-purpose flour (see p. 17)

2 tablespoons chopped fresh parsley, to garnish

1. Remove any excess fat and then cut the beef into long slices, ½ in (1 cm) thick.
2. Melt the lard in a large saucepan, add the onions, and fry until golden brown.
3. Add the slices of beef, marjoram, salt, and pepper, and cook for a few minutes, stirring very frequently.
4. Stir in the wine and simmer gently for about 15 minutes.
5. Meanwhile, cut the bacon into strips and fry in a small frying pan for a few minutes; then add to the stew, together with the garlic.
6. Add a few tablespoons of the hot sauce to the yogurt and then stir the yogurt slowly into the stew.
7. Continue to simmer gently for 20 to 30 minutes or until the meat is tender.
8. Serve garnished with the parsley and accompanied by boiled potatoes or a rice pilaf.

rama's bath

I find fascinating, not only the name of this dish, but also the fact that it is the only recipe incorporating yogurt that I have been able to trace from Thailand. I suspect that it is a dish of Indian origin that has been taken over and adapted by the Thais.

COCONUT MILK

4 cups coconut milk (canned, or made from dried; see below)

PASTE MIXTURE

3 garlic cloves

3 scallions

1 teaspoon roughly chopped ginger

3 fresh chili peppers

1 tablespoon lime or lemon juice

salt to taste

1 lb (½ kg) beef steak

1 tablespoon brown sugar

1 tablespoon finely chopped roasted nuts (e.g. peanuts, almonds, or walnuts)

1 tablespoon soy sauce

2 tablespoons flour

1 teaspoon salt

1 lb (½ kg) fresh or frozen spinach

⅔–1¼ cups (150–300 ml) yogurt, depending on taste

TO MAKE COCONUT MILK (A SIMPLIFIED RECIPE)

1. Soak ½ lb (250 g) dried shredded coconut in 1¼ cups (300 ml) water for about 10 minutes.
2. Strain off the liquid and retain it.
3. Repeat steps 1 and 2 twice more.
4. When you have almost 4 cups (1 l) of the liquid, boil it in a saucepan for about 10 minutes until it is reduced slightly.

TO MAKE THE PASTE MIXTURE

1. Put all the ingredients in a blender or food processor and blend until smooth.
2. Cut the meat into ½ in (1 cm) slices.
3. Put the coconut milk, sugar, nuts, and soy sauce into a large saucepan.

4. Add the meat, bring to a boil, then lower the heat and simmer for about 30 minutes.
5. Mix the flour to a smooth paste with a little water and stir into the saucepan.
6. Add the paste mixture to the pan, stir thoroughly, season with salt, cover, and simmer until the meat is tender and the sauce has thickened, about 40 to 50 minutes.
7. If using fresh spinach, wash it thoroughly. If using frozen spinach, thaw it out.
8. Half-fill a large pan with boiling salted water, add the spinach, and cook for 5 to 10 minutes.
9. Drain the spinach, squeeze out excess moisture, and arrange on a serving plate.
10. Spoon the meat and sauce over the spinach and pour the yogurt over the top.
11. Serve immediately with a plain rice pilaf.

madznov hortimiss

BEEF WITH YOGURT

This Armenian dish is usually made with sour cream, but I think that yogurt adds an extra dimension to the flavor. Traditionally, pickled grapes and apples are served as a garnish or side dish. Serve with a pilaf of your choice.

2 lb (1 kg) beef, fillet or sirloin
1 teaspoon salt
½ teaspoon black pepper
4 tablespoons (2 oz/50 g) ghee
    or unsalted butter
1 teaspoon ground cloves

2½ cups (600 ml) yogurt, stabilized
    with 1 egg or 1 tablespoon all-
    purpose flour (see p. 17)
1 tablespoon sumac
pickled apples and pickled grapes,
    to garnish

1. Trim the beef of all fat and gristle.
2. Cut the beef into ½ in (1 cm) slices and pound thin with a mallet.
3. Sprinkle the meat with the salt and pepper.
4. Melt the ghee in a large pan and sauté the meat slices quickly over a moderate heat for 1 to 2 minutes only, turning once.
5. Sprinkle the meat with the cloves, add the yogurt, and toss gently.
6. Cover the pan and simmer for about 10 to 15 minutes.
7. Transfer the meat to a large shallow dish, pour the sauce over the top, sprinkle with the sumac, and serve immediately.
8. Garnish with the pickled apples and grapes and serve.

dry beef curry

A curry to eat with *chapatis* rather than rice. It may be made with lamb instead of beef, but should then be cooked for 45 minutes to 1 hour.

¼ cup vegetable oil

2 green chilis, finely chopped

2 onions, finely chopped

2 lb (1 kg) beef steak, cut into
 ½ in (1 cm) cubes

½ teaspoon salt

2 tomatoes, blanched, peeled,
 and chopped

1 teaspoon turmeric

1 teaspoon cumin

2 teaspoons ground coriander

1½ teaspoons *garam masala*

1¼ cups (300 ml) stabilized yogurt
 (see p. 17)

1 tablespoon chopped fresh cilantro

1. Heat the oil in a saucepan, add the chilis, and fry for 1 minute.
2. Add the onions and fry until soft, but not brown.
3. Add the beef cubes and salt and fry, stirring frequently, until the meat is browned on all sides.
4. Reduce the heat and add the tomatoes.
5. Continue cooking for 10 minutes or until most of the tomato liquid has evaporated.
6. In a small bowl combine the turmeric, cumin, ground coriander, and 1 teaspoon of the *garam masala*.
7. Add the yogurt and continue beating until yogurt and spices are well blended.
8. Add this to the meat mixture in the saucepan and stir well.
9. Half cover the pan, reduce heat to low, and simmer the curry for 1½ hours.
10. Remove the lid from the pan and continue cooking for a further 30 minutes or until the liquid has evaporated, leaving the meat in a thick sauce.
11. If it becomes too dry, cover the pan and continue cooking.
12. Spoon the curry into a serving dish and sprinkle the top with the remaining *garam masala* and chopped cilantro.

borani-ye goosht

LENTIL STEW WITH YOGURT

This is a typical Middle Eastern stew with the added Iranian touches of saffron and oregano. It is equally delicious hot or cold, so you can serve it as an hors d'oeuvre or as a main dish.

1 large eggplant
2 tablespoons (1 oz/25 g) butter
1 onion, finely chopped
1 lb (½ kg) shoulder of lamb,
  cut into small pieces
2½ cups (600 ml) stock
1 teaspoon salt
½ teaspoon black pepper

½ teaspoon saffron diluted in
  1 tablespoon hot water
1 teaspoon dried oregano
3 oz (75 g) whole brown lentils,
  rinsed
2½ cups (600 ml) yogurt
1 garlic clove, finely chopped

1. Peel the eggplant, cut in half lengthwise, and then cut crosswise into ¼ in (½ cm) slices.
2. Melt the butter in a large saucepan and sauté the onion until golden brown.
3. Add the meat and cook for a few minutes, turning frequently.
4. Add the stock, salt, pepper, saffron, and oregano and bring to a boil.
5. Cover and simmer for 1 hour.
6. Add the lentils and the eggplant slices to the pan, cover, and simmer for a further 30 to 40 minutes or until all the ingredients are very tender. Add more water if necessary.
8. At this stage you can serve the stew with the yogurt stirred through it.
9. However, it is traditional to cool the stew slightly and then blend it or pound it to a paste in a large mortar and pestle.
10. The yogurt is then stirred into the pulp and the garlic is sprinkled over the top.
11. Serve cold with bread (e.g. pita) or hot with a rice pilaf.

korma

This Indian dish has a delicate flavor, yet is full of fascinating spices. Serve with a plain rice pilaf.

2 onions
1 tablespoon chopped fresh ginger
1 garlic clove
½ teaspoon ground cumin
¼ teaspoon ground cardamom
¼ teaspoon ground cloves
4 tablespoons (2 oz/50 g) butter
2 teaspoons salt
½ teaspoon ground saffron
1 oz (25 g) cashew nuts

4 dried chilis, seeds removed
  and discarded
2 teaspoons ground coriander
2 lb (1 kg) leg of lamb, cut into
  1 in (3 cm) pieces
generous ½ cup (150 ml)
  stabilized yogurt (see p. 17)
2 tablespoons chopped cilantro or
  parsley

1. Peel the onions, slice one, and chop the other finely.
2. Put the chopped onion into a blender with the ginger, garlic, cashew nuts, chilis, coriander, cumin, cardamom, cloves, and a generous ½ cup (150 ml) water, and blend until smooth.
3. Melt the butter in a large saucepan or casserole, add the sliced onion, and cook until golden brown.
4. Add the blended spices, a generous ½ cup (150 ml) water, and the salt, and continue cooking until much of the liquid has evaporated.
5. Add the meat and mix well until the meat cubes are well coated with the spices.
6. Mix the saffron with 2 to 3 tablespoons of boiling water and steep for a few minutes.
7. Stir the saffron into the meat mixture.
8. Add the yogurt and mix thoroughly.
9. Reduce the heat, cover, and simmer for about 1 hour until the meat is very tender. Stir occasionally to prevent sticking.
10. Sprinkle with the cilantro or parsley and cook for a further 5 minutes.
11. Spoon into a dish and serve immediately.

roghan josh

LAMB IN YOGURT AND SPICES

Kashmiri dishes make great use of yogurt. There are several recipes for *roghan josh*, but this is my favorite—an added bonus is that it is a little simpler to prepare than some of the others. *Chapatis, parathas*, or even pita bread will make an excellent accompaniment.

1¼ cups (300 ml) yogurt
2 tablespoons (1 oz/25 g) ghee
   or butter, melted
2 teaspoons salt
1 teaspoon ground ginger
2 lb (1 kg) lean lamb, cut into
   1 in (3 cm) pieces

1½ teaspoons chili powder
1 teaspoon ground cumin
2 teaspoons *garam masala*
2 tablespoons chopped fresh
   cilantro (optional)

1. Mix the yogurt, ghee, salt, and ginger together in a large saucepan.
2. Add the meat cubes, turn until they are well coated, and then cover and simmer for a few minutes, stirring occasionally.
3. After about 5 minutes you will notice that the juices are evaporating. Stir in about ½ cup (150 ml) water, together with the chili powder and cumin.
4. Simmer for about 10 to 15 minutes, stirring frequently, until the water has evaporated.
5. Add a little more water and simmer for a further 10 to 15 minutes.
6. Continue cooking the meat in this way until it is tender.
7. Add the *garam masala* and cilantro, stir, and simmer for another 10 to 15 minutes, stirring very frequently.
8. Pile onto a large plate and serve immediately.

jagnjeca kapama s jajima

LAMB AND EGG CASSEROLE

This is a dish from Serbia; it owes its origin to the Turkish Ottoman domination of that country. It is a rich, tasty stew and looks attractive on a dinner table with its golden crust. Serve with boiled potatoes or pita bread.

1½ lb (¾ kg) boned leg of lamb, cut into 1 in (3 cm) pieces
salt and pepper to taste
1 large leek, trimmed—leaving some of the tender green part— washed carefully, and chopped

2 tablespoons flour
¼ cup olive oil
1 large onion, finely chopped
1¼ cups (300 ml) water or stock
2–3 eggs
1¼ cups (300 ml) yogurt

1. Preheat the oven to 325°F (160°C).
2. Sprinkle some salt and pepper over the meat cubes and coat them with the flour.
3. Heat the oil in a large casserole and fry the lamb cubes, turning frequently, until they are browned all over.
4. With a slotted spoon remove the meat cubes and transfer to a plate.
5. Add the onion and leek to the pan and fry, stirring occasionally for about 10 minutes.
6. Return the meat to the pan and stir in the water or stock.
7. Bring to a boil, cover, and place in the oven for about 1½ hours or until the meat is tender.
8. Beat the eggs thoroughly into the yogurt and then pour it into the casserole.
9. Return to the oven and cook for a further 30 minutes or until it is golden and set firm.

badami gosht

LAMB WITH SAFFRON AND ALMONDS

This recipe from northern India is undoubtedly Iranian in origin. It is a most attractive and beautifully colored dish, which is very spicy but by no means hot.

A saffron rice pilaf is an excellent accompaniment, as is *jajig*—the yogurt and cucumber salad on p. 92.

½ teaspoon saffron strands soaked in 2 tablespoons hot water

1¼ cups (300 ml) yogurt, stabilized with 1 egg or 1 tablespoon all-purpose flour (see p. 17)

1½ teaspoons salt

2 lb (1 kg) boned lamb, excess fat removed and the meat cut into 1 in (3 cm) cubes

4 tablespoons (2 oz/50 g) ghee or butter

1 small cinnamon stick

3 whole cloves

1 onion, finely chopped

2 garlic cloves, finely chopped

1 teaspoon grated fresh ginger

1 teaspoon ground cumin

3 cardamom pods (optional)

1½ tablespoons ground almonds

1 tablespoon chopped fresh mint

1. Squeeze the saffron strands in their water to release as much of the color and fragrance as possible.
2. Put the yogurt into a large bowl and stir in the saffron water and salt.
3. Add the meat cubes, turn until coated with the mixture, and set aside.
4. In a large saucepan or casserole, melt the ghee, add the cinnamon stick and cloves, and fry for a few minutes.
5. Add the onion, garlic, and ginger, and fry gently for a few minutes until the onions are golden brown.
6. Now add the cumin and fry for 2 more minutes.
7. Drain the pieces of meat but reserve the marinade. Add the meat to the pan and toss in the spices until well coated.
8. Stir in the yogurt marinade, almonds, cardamom pods, and 1¼ cups (300 ml) water, lower the heat, and simmer for about 1 hour or until the lamb is tender and the sauce is thick. Stir frequently to prevent the meat from sticking.
9. Stir in the mint and serve immediately on a bed of rice pilaf.

tah chin

BAKED RICE AND LAMB CASSEROLE

This dish, the name of which literally means "arranged on the bottom of the pan," is one of the great classics of Iranian cuisine. It makes a wholesome meal and is very attractive in appearance.

SERVES SIX

2 cups (450 ml) yogurt
1 large onion, sliced
1 teaspoon saffron
1 tablespoon lemon juice
1 teaspoon salt
½ teaspoon black pepper
2–3 lb (1–1½ kg) leg of lamb, boned

2 tablespoons salt
1 lb (500 g) basmati rice,
  washed thoroughly
2 egg yolks
6 tablespoons (3 oz/75 g) butter,
  melted

1. In a large bowl, mix together the yogurt, onion, half the saffron, lemon juice, salt, and pepper.
2. Add the meat, turn to ensure it is well coated, and then leave to marinate overnight.
3. Preheat the oven to 350°F (180°C).
4. Remove the meat from the marinade, place in a roasting pan, and bake for about 2 hours, or until tender. Reserve the marinade.
5. Allow the meat to cool and then cut into thick slices.
6. Three-quarters fill a large saucepan with water and bring to a boil.
7. Add the 2 tablespoons of salt and pour in the rice slowly so that the water does not stop boiling. Stir once.
8. Boil for 6 minutes, drain into a colander, rinse with cold water, and drain again.
9. Put half of the rice into a bowl and mix in the marinade and the egg yolks.
10. Put half the melted butter in the bottom of a saucepan and then spread the rice mixture over the bottom of the pan.
11. Arrange the slices of meat over the rice and then cover with the remaining rice.

12. Place a dish towel over the top of the pan and then fit on the lid.
13. Steam over a very low heat for about 45 minutes.
14. Dissolve the remaining saffron in 1 tablespoon of hot water.
15. Remove ¼ cup of the cooked rice from the top of the pan, place in a small bowl, add the saffron mixture, and stir until the rice is golden.
16. Empty out the rice and meat on to a large serving plate, garnish with the saffron rice, and pour the remaining melted butter over the top.
17. There will be a thick, crisp crust of rice (*tah-dig*) at the bottom of the pan. To remove it in one piece, stand the pan in 2 in (5 cm) cold water for 2 to 3 minutes and then lift out with a spatula. Cut into pieces and arrange around the edge of the serving plate.

banja a jagnjetinom

LAMB AND OKRA CASSEROLE WITH YOGURT

Okra—or ladies' fingers—is a popular Indo-Iranian vegetable that has spread throughout the Middle East. This dish is popular, in one form or another, throughout the Balkans and Near and Middle East. Yogurt is an essential accompaniment.

1 lb (½ kg) fresh okra
juice of 1 lemon
¼ cup olive or vegetable oil
1 onion, finely chopped
1½ lb (¾ kg) lamb cut into 1 in (3 cm) pieces
1 heaped tablespoon flour
½ teaspoon black pepper

¼ teaspoon cayenne pepper
1 teaspoon salt
2 tablespoons finely chopped parsley
2–3 large tomatoes, blanched, peeled, and sliced
2½ cups (600 ml) garlic yogurt sauce (see p. 247)

1. Wash the okra and remove the stem by cutting the thin cone-shaped skin off the top—take care not to cut through the shell of the vegetable or the juice will run out.
2. Put the okra into a bowl and sprinkle with a little salt and a little of the lemon juice.
3. Shake the bowl to mix well.
4. Heat the oil in a large casserole, add the onion and the meat cubes, and fry, turning frequently, until golden brown.
5. Stir in the flour, black and cayenne peppers, salt, parsley, and 1¼ cups (300 ml) water.
6. Bring to a boil, lower the heat, and simmer, covered, for about 1 hour or until the meat is just tender.
7. Add the okra, the rest of the lemon juice, and the tomatoes; stir gently and then simmer, uncovered, for a further ½ hour or until the okra is tender. Take care not to overcook or the okra will lose its shape.
8. Serve immediately, with the garlic yogurt sauce in a separate bowl.

raan

ROAST LEG OF LAMB IN YOGURT

This is a delightful Kashmiri dish. The meat is full of flavor and it is best served with plain rice pilaf and a garnish of sliced cucumber and tomatoes.

1 leg of lamb, approximately
   3–4 lb (1½–2 kg), boned and excess
   fat removed
1 teaspoon grated fresh ginger
2 garlic cloves, finely chopped
2 teaspoons salt
½ teaspoon ground cumin
½ teaspoon turmeric
½ teaspoon cinnamon
½ teaspoon ground cardamom

½ teaspoon chili powder
1 tablespoon lemon juice
1 tablespoon olive oil
generous ½ cup (150 ml) yogurt
1 tablespoon blanched almonds
1 tablespoon pistachios or cashews
¼ teaspoon ground saffron
2 teaspoons honey
cucumber and tomato slices, to
   garnish, optional

1. Make several deep incisions all over the leg of lamb.
2. Mix together in a bowl the ginger, garlic, salt, cumin, turmeric, cinnamon, cardamom, chili powder, lemon juice, and olive oil.
3. Rub this mixture over the lamb, especially into the slits.
4. Put the yogurt, almonds, nuts, saffron, and honey into a blender or food processor and blend.
5. Place the lamb in a deep dish and pour the yogurt mixture over it.
6. Cover and leave for 6 to 8 hours or overnight in the refrigerator. Spread marinade over meat before and during marination.
7. Turn the lamb once or twice while it is marinating.
8. Preheat oven to 350°F (180°C).
9. Place the lamb and any remaining marinade in a roasting dish and cook for approximately 2 hours or until cooked through. Transfer to a plate.
10. Garnish with the tomato and cucumber slices and serve with a plain pilaf.

khorak-e-kashk-bademjan

EGGPLANT CASSEROLE

This is a popular Iranian dish from the region of Kerman. It was traditionally made with *kashk*, liquid whey, but nowadays yogurt is almost always used instead. Yellow split peas, turmeric, and walnuts give it an exotic flavor. It is always accompanied by a bowl of rice pilaf.

6 tablespoons (3 oz/75 g) ghee
  or butter
2 onions, thinly sliced
1½ lb (¾ kg) lean lamb, cut into
  pieces
½ teaspoon black pepper
2 oz (50 g) split peas, soaked
  overnight in cold water
1 eggplant

2½ cups (600 ml) stock
1 teaspoon salt
1½ tablespoons tomato paste mixed
  with a generous ½ cup (150 ml)
  warm water
1¼ cups (300 ml) yogurt
½ teaspoon turmeric
1 oz (25 g) chopped walnuts

1. Melt 2 tablespoons (1 oz/25 g) ghee or butter in a large saucepan.
2. Add the onions and fry until soft and golden brown.
3. Add the pieces of meat and fry, stirring frequently, until brown all over.
4. Stir in the stock, salt, pepper, and diluted tomato paste.
5. Bring to a boil, cover, and simmer for about 45 minutes.
6. Add the split peas and cook for a further 15 to 20 minutes or until peas are just tender.
7. Preheat the oven to 350°F (180°C).
8. Meanwhile, cut the top off the eggplant and peel it.
9. Cut it in half lengthwise and slice crosswise into ¼ in (½ cm) pieces.
10. If desired, place the slices on a plate, sprinkle with salt, and leave for 30 minutes. Rinse the pieces under cold water and dry on paper towels.
11. Melt the remaining 4 tablespoons (2 oz/50 g) butter in a large frying pan and sauté the eggplant slices until they are brown on both sides.

12. Drain on paper towels to remove excess fat.
13. Pour the meat and pea mixture into a baking dish and arrange the eggplant slices over the top.
14. Bake for about 40 minutes.
15. Mix the yogurt and turmeric together in a small bowl. Stir in 2 or 3 tablespoons of the hot sauce and then pour over the meat and eggplants.
16. Sprinkle with the walnuts and serve immediately.

kourza

DUMPLINGS STUFFED WITH MEAT

This is a Caucasian recipe from Azerbaijan related to *manti*—a ravioli-type dumpling—which is characteristic of Mongolian cuisine. The dumplings were usually made in advance and cooked whenever the nomads had time to stop. It is a convenient and versatile dish as it can be made into a soup—as with *mantabour* (see p. 53)—or a main dish as here.

DOUGH
8 oz (250 g) all-purpose flour
2 eggs
pinch of salt

FILLING
2 tablespoons (1 oz/25 g) butter
½ lb (250 g) ground lamb or beef

1 onion, finely chopped
1 teaspoon salt
½ teaspoon black pepper
½ teaspoon cinnamon

2½ cups (600 ml) yogurt
1 garlic clove (optional)

1. For the dough: place the flour in a large mixing bowl and make a hollow in the middle. Add the eggs, ¼ cup of water, and the salt.
2. Mix the ingredients together until a dough is formed. Add a little more water if necessary.
3. Form the dough into a ball.
4. Sprinkle some flour on to a work surface and then knead the dough for 10 to 15 minutes, adding a little more flour if the dough becomes sticky.
5. Cover with a dish towel and leave to rest for about 30 minutes.
6. Meanwhile, melt the butter in a saucepan, add the meat and onion, and sauté until the meat turns dark brown, stirring frequently.
7. Season with the salt and pepper and remove from the heat.
8. For convenience, divide the dough into two or three balls.
9. Roll out one of the balls on a floured surface until paper thin.
10. Cut out as many 3 in (8 cm) circles as possible.

12. Repeat with the remaining balls of dough.
13. Place about 1 teaspoon of the meat mixture in the lower half of each circle of dough.
14. Dip a finger in cold water and run it around the edge of the circle.
15. Fold the top half over the lower half to make a half moon.
16. Seal the edges with the prongs of a fork.
17. In a large saucepan, boil some water with 1 teaspoon of salt.
18. Drop in some of the dumplings, about six or eight at a time, and simmer for about 10 minutes or until the dumplings rise to the surface.
19. Transfer the cooked dumplings to paper towels to drain and then keep them warm.
20. Repeat until all the dumplings are cooked.
21. Place all the dumplings in a large serving dish and sprinkle with the cinnamon.
22. Serve accompanied by a bowl of yogurt flavored with the garlic, if desired.

kutab

LAMB PASTRIES

This popular recipe from the Caucasus is actually of Mongolian origin. The pastries are fried in butter and served with sumac and yogurt. A fresh mixed salad is all you need to accompany this dish.

DOUGH
8 oz (250 g) all-purpose flour
2 eggs
pinch of salt

FILLING
½ lb (250 g) ground lamb
1 small onion, finely chopped
2 tablespoons fresh pomegranate

juice or 1 teaspoon commercial
concentrated pomegranate juice
pinch of cinnamon
salt and pepper to taste

1–1½ cups (150-300 ml) vegetable oil
2 tablespoons sumac
2 cups (450 ml) yogurt

1. First prepare the dough. Place the flour in a large mixing bowl and make a hollow in the middle.
2. Add the eggs, ¼ cup of water, and the salt.
3. Mix the ingredients together until a dough is formed. Add a little more water if necessary.
4. Form the dough into a ball.
5. Sprinkle some flour on a flat work surface and knead the dough for 10 to 15 minutes, adding a little more flour if it becomes sticky.
6. Cover with a dish towel and leave to rest for 30 minutes.
7. Meanwhile, in a large bowl, combine all the filling ingredients and knead until well blended and smooth.
8. For convenience, divide the dough into two balls.
9. Roll out one of the balls on a floured surface until paper thin.
10. Cut into circles 3 in (8 cm) in diameter.
11. Repeat with the remaining ball of dough.
12. Place a teaspoon of the meat mixture in the lower half of each dough circle.

13. Dip a finger in cold water and run it around the edge of the circle.
14. Fold the top half over the lower half to make a half moon.
15. Seal the edges with the prongs of a fork.
16. In a large frying pan or saucepan, heat the vegetable oil.
17. Add a few of the pastries and fry gently until golden brown. Do not fry too quickly or the meat inside will not be cooked.
18. Cook the remaining pastries in the same way, keeping those already cooked warm in the oven. You may find it necessary to add more oil from time to time.
19. Serve all the pastries on a large plate with the sumac sprinkled over the top.
20. Either serve the yogurt in a separate bowl or spooned over the pastries.

VARIATION

In Azerbaijan steamed and puréed pumpkin is often used as a filling.

1 small pumpkin, 2–3 lb (1–1½ kg)	2 tablespoons fresh pomegranate
1 onion, finely chopped	juice or 1 teaspoon concentrated
½ teaspoon cinnamon	juice
salt and pepper to taste	

1. Remove the skin and seeds from the pumpkin as you would from a melon.
2. Cut the flesh into small pieces.
3. Place in a large saucepan with 1½ teaspoons of salt and sufficient water to cover.
4. Bring to a boil and simmer until very soft.
5. Drain and mash the pumpkin to a purée.
6. Fry the onion in a little vegetable oil until soft.
7. Place the pumpkin purée in a large bowl with the fried onion, pomegranate juice, cinnamon, and salt and pepper to taste.
8. Mix together and then proceed to make the pastries as described above.

poultry

dami ghalebi ba morgh

RICE WITH CHICKEN AND DRIED FRUIT

This Iranian dish is very decorative as well as delicious. Traditionally it is cooked in a mold and then inverted onto a serving platter to show a golden brown crust. However it can be layered in a casserole and baked in the oven or steamed in a saucepan over a low heat. Salads and yogurt drinks make ideal accompaniments.

4 large prunes, pitted

8 dates, pitted

8 dried apricots

8 dried peaches (optional)

12 oz (350 g) long-grain rice, washed thoroughly under cold running water and drained

2 teaspoons salt

4 chicken breasts, washed and dried

1 onion, thinly sliced

generous ½ cup (150 ml) chicken stock or water

1 teaspoon salt

½ teaspoon black pepper

8 tablespoons (4 oz/100 g) butter, melted

½ teaspoon saffron

generous ½ cup (150 ml) yogurt

2 oz (50 g) chopped walnuts

2 oz (50 g) raisins

1. Cut the prunes, dates, apricots, and peaches into small pieces, place in a bowl of cold water, and set aside.
2. Place 3½ cups (1 l) water and 2 teaspoons salt in a large saucepan and bring to a boil.
3. Add the rice and simmer for about 20 minutes or until all the water has been absorbed.
4. Meanwhile, place the chicken breasts in a large saucepan with the onion, stock, salt, and pepper.
5. Cover and simmer for about 30 minutes, or until tender, turning occasionally.

6. Remove the chicken from the pan, reserving the stock. Let it cool to the touch and remove and discard the bones.

7. Drain the dried fruit.

8. If you will use a mold or casserole, preheat the oven to 375°F (190°C).

9. In a small bowl, mix together 4 tablespoons (2 oz/50 g) melted butter, the saffron, the yogurt, and 1 cup of the cooked rice.

10. If using a mold, grease it with butter and then coat its entire surface with the yogurt mixture. If using a casserole or saucepan, line the bottom with the mixture. Over this mixture, arrange first a layer of plain rice, then some dried fruit, some chicken pieces, some of the chopped walnuts and raisins, and 1 to 2 teaspoons of the stock. Continue alternating layers until the receptacle is full, ending with a layer of rice.

11. Mix the remaining melted butter and chicken stock together and pour over the top layer of rice.

12. Bake for about 1 hour, or, if using a saucepan, place it over a low heat, wrap the lid in a dish towel, and place firmly on the pan. Steam for about 30 to 45 minutes.

13. To unmold, dip up to the rim in cold water for a couple of minutes and then invert on to a large serving dish.

dapakhav madznov

FRIED CHICKEN WITH PRUNE AND YOGURT SAUCE

This is a classic Caucasian recipe. It is known among Georgians as *tabaka* and among Armenians as *dabakadz hav*. I have adapted it very slightly to incorporate yogurt and to my delight have found that it works beautifully.

4 young Cornish game hens (1–1½ lb/
  500–700 g), washed and dried
2 tablespoons salt
½ cup (150 ml) yogurt

6 tablespoons (3 oz/75 g)
  ghee or butter
3 tomatoes, thinly sliced
1 small eggplant, cut in half

lengthwise and then cut crosswise
into ¼ in (½ cm) slices
1 garlic clove, crushed

½ teaspoon ground cinnamon
½–1¼ cups (150–300 ml)
tkemali sauce (see p. 253)

1. Place a hen on a chopping board, back upwards.
2. With a sharp pointed knife, start at the neck and cut along one side of the backbone.
3. Turn the hen around and cut along the other side of the backbone, freeing it.
4. Break it away from the spoon-shaped bone connecting the breasts and remove both the bones and the white cartilage.
5. Loosen the skin around the leg and thigh and push it back, exposing the thigh joint. Cut it half across and pull the skin back. Repeat with the other leg.
6. Make a small slit in each breast below the ribs.
7. Turn the hen flesh side down, cover with wax paper, and then flatten with a meat mallet.
8. Twist the legs inwards and push them through the holes in the breasts.
9. Repeat with each hen.
10. Rub the hens with the salt and spread the flesh sides evenly with half the yogurt.
11. Melt 4 tablespoons (2 oz/50 g) of the butter in a large frying pan, add two hens skin side down, place a heavy weight on top, and cook over a moderate heat for 8 to 10 minutes.
12. Turn the hens over, spread with half the remaining yogurt, weigh down, and fry for a further 10 minutes until golden brown, being careful not to burn them.
13. Repeat with the two remaining hens, keeping the first two warm.
14. Meanwhile, melt the remaining 2 tablespoons (1 oz/25 g) butter in a saucepan and sauté the tomatoes, eggplant, garlic, and cinnamon until soft.
15. Serve one Cornish game hen per person, accompanied by some of the cooked vegetables and the *tkemali* sauce.

nourov jud

CHICKEN WITH POMEGRANATES

This is one of my family's specialties. It is simple and economical to make and looks stunning on the dinner table when decorated with the red pomegranate seeds. It is also very tasty!

1 chicken (about 3 lb/1½ kg)
4 tablespoons (2 oz/50 g) butter
1 teaspoon salt
½ teaspoon black pepper
½ teaspoon ground cumin
seeds from 2 pomegranates

1 onion, thinly sliced
1¼ cups (300 ml) chicken stock
2½ cups (600 ml) yogurt, stabilized
    with 1 egg or 1 tablespoon all-
    purpose flour (see p. 17)

1. Wash and dry the chicken and cut into eight serving pieces.
2. Melt the butter in a large saucepan and sauté the onion until golden brown.
3. Add the chicken pieces, stock, salt, pepper, and cumin, and bring to a boil.
4. Cover and simmer for about 45 minutes or until tender, turning occasionally.
5. When ready to serve, remove from the heat and spoon a few tablespoons of the hot sauce into the yogurt.
6. Gently stir the yogurt into the saucepan and just heat through but do not boil.
7. Arrange the chicken in a serving dish, pour the sauce over the top, and then sprinkle the red pomegranate seeds all over it.

souryani chicken

ASSYRIAN CHICKEN WITH YOGURT

Assyrians—what is left of that mighty nation—still survive in parts of the Middle East and though now ignored and forgotten by others, they retain their age-old culture and customs. I was given this recipe by an Assyrian friend from Baghdad. It is a very old recipe, although it has, no doubt, been extensively modernized with the passing of time.

1 roasting chicken (about 3 lb/ 1½ kg), cut into 8 serving pieces

4 tablespoons (2 oz/50 g) butter or ghee

1 onion, finely chopped

1 green pepper, finely sliced

2 tablespoons sumac

2½ cups (600 ml) chicken stock

1 teaspoon salt

½ teaspoon black pepper

2 tablespoons ground almonds

1¼ cups (300 ml) yogurt

1 teaspoon cayenne pepper

1 teaspoon ground cumin

1. Melt the butter or ghee in a large saucepan and cook the chicken pieces until golden brown on all sides.
2. Remove the chicken pieces from the pan to a large plate and keep warm.
3. Add the onion and green pepper to the pan and sauté for a few minutes until the onion is soft and translucent. Add the stock, sumac, salt, and pepper.
4. Return the chicken pieces to the saucepan; cover, lower the heat, and simmer for 40 to 60 minutes until the chicken is tender.
5. Transfer the chicken pieces to a serving dish and keep warm.
6. Add a few tablespoons of water to the ground almonds, stir to a smooth paste, and add to the juices in the pan. Bring to a boil, stirring all the time.
7. Turn off the heat and add the yogurt to the sauce, stirring all the time.
8. Pour the sauce over the chicken and garnish with the cayenne pepper and cumin.
9. Serve with an accompaniment of a rice or bulgar pilaf.

murgh tikka

SKEWERED CHICKEN

An easy way to cook chicken. It is a must in all Indian restaurants, and is traditionally served with an onion and tomato salad and *chapatis*.

2 lb (1 kg) boneless, skinless chicken breasts or thighs
1 onion, roughly chopped
2 garlic cloves, roughly chopped
4 teaspoons finely chopped fresh ginger
juice of 1 large lemon

1¼ cups (300 ml) yogurt
2 teaspoons ground coriander
½ teaspoon ground cumin
2 teaspoons salt
3 tablespoons chopped fresh cilantro or mint

2. Cut the chicken flesh into 1 in (3 cm) pieces.
3. In a blender, blend the onion, garlic, ginger, and lemon juice until smooth.
4. Empty this paste into a large bowl; add the yogurt, coriander, cumin, and salt, and mix well.
5. Add the chicken pieces, turn until well coated, and leave to marinate at room temperature for a few hours or in the refrigerator overnight.
6. Thread the pieces of meat on to skewers and cook on a grill or under the broiler for 10 to 12 minutes, turning frequently.
7. Sprinkle with the chopped cilantro or mint and serve immediately with a rice pilaf of your choice or with *chapatis*.

tandoori murgh

CHICKEN TANDOORI

Tandoori chicken is a north Indian dish, spread throughout the world in the last few years by countless tandoori restaurants. Traditionally, the chicken is cooked in a *tandoor* (similar to the Turkish *tandir* and the Armenian *tonir*)—a cylindrical clay oven still popular in the remote villages of the Caucasus, Iran, and Turkey, as well as India. In a modern kitchen, tandoori chicken can be cooked in the oven or on the grill.

1 chicken, about 3 lb (1½ kg),
  skin removed
1 teaspoon cayenne pepper
2 tablespoons lemon juice
salt and pepper to taste

MARINADE
3–4 in (8–10 cm) piece fresh ginger,
  peeled and chopped

4 garlic cloves, crushed
2 teaspoons whole coriander seeds
1 tablespoon ground cumin
2 tablespoons lemon juice
3 tablespoons yogurt
1 tablespoon cayenne pepper
1 teaspoon red vegetable coloring
3 tablespoons (1½ oz/40 g) ghee
  or butter, melted

1. Wash the chicken thoroughly and dry with paper towel.
2. In a small bowl, mix the cayenne pepper, lemon juice, salt, and black pepper together and rub the mixture all over the chicken.
3. Set aside for 45 minutes.
4. Meanwhile, make the marinade by mixing all the ingredients together in a large bowl.
5. Place the chicken in the bowl and coat generously with the marinade.
6. Cover and refrigerate for 12 to 18 hours.
7. Remove the chicken, drain, and thread whole onto a large skewer. If you find it easier, cut it in half and thread the halves onto two skewers. (In this case the cooking time will be 30 to 45 minutes.)

8. Cook over on the grill, turning and basting regularly with the marinade so that it does not burn. Alternatively, roast it in the oven at 350°F (180°C) for 1 to 1½ hours or until cooked through. (Test by sticking the point of a sharp knife into the thigh.)

9. Serve immediately on a large platter garnished with thinly sliced onions, tomatoes, and chopped chili peppers, all dressed with lemon juice.

10. Accompany with *chapatis* or *naan* bread.

kinov hav

DRUNKEN CHICKEN

What a wonderful description! I need add no more. Boiled or roast potatoes or a
rice or bulgar pilaf make good accompaniments.

1 chicken (about 3 lb/1½ kg)
seasoned flour—you can vary the
  ingredients, but basically they
  are: 2 oz (50 g) flour, ½ teaspoon
  black pepper, ½ teaspoon dried
  marjoram, 1 teaspoon salt, ½
  teaspoon fenugreek

4 tablespoons (2 oz/50 g) butter
generous ½ cup (150 ml) brandy
2½ cups (600 ml) yogurt, stabilized
  with 2 eggs (see p. 17)
2 teaspoons paprika
a few sprigs of parsley

1. Preheat the oven to 350°F (180°C).
2. Clean, wash, dry, and cut the chicken into eight serving pieces.
3. Mix the seasoned flour on a large plate and roll the chicken pieces in it.
4. Melt the butter in a large ovenproof casserole.
5. Add the chicken and brown on all sides.
6. Add the brandy and cover.
7. Cook in the middle of the oven for about 1 hour or until the chicken is tender.
   Baste regularly with the juices. If you like a crisp skin then remove the cover
   of the dish for the last 10 to 15 minutes.
8. Pour in the stabilized yogurt and cook over a low heat for a further 5 minutes.
9. Transfer to a serving dish, pour the sauce over the top, and sprinkle with
   the paprika.
10. Serve immediately, garnished with the parsley.

khorsht-e mast

CHICKEN IN ORANGE AND YOGURT SAUCE

This Iranian dish can also be prepared with lamb—use 2 lb (1 kg) lean lamb, boned and cut into 1½ in (4 cm) pieces. The attractive creamy sauce has a delicate, tangy flavor. Serve with a plain rice pilaf.

1 chicken, about 3 lb (1½ kg),
  cut into 8 pieces
2 tablespoons (1 oz/25 g) butter
2 small onions, thinly sliced
2½ cups (600 ml) chicken stock
½ teaspoon black pepper

1 teaspoon salt
½ teaspoon saffron
zest of one orange
2 cups (450 ml) yogurt, stabilized
  with 1 egg (see p. 17)

1. In a large heavy-based saucepan or casserole, melt the butter and sauté the onions until they are golden brown.
2. Stir in the stock, salt, pepper, and saffron.
3. Add the chicken pieces, turn in the stock, cover, and simmer for about an hour or until tender. Turn the pieces at least once so that they are cooked all over.
4. Stir in the orange zest and simmer, uncovered, for a further 20 minutes.
5. Pour the stabilized yogurt into a small bowl and stir in a few tablespoons of the hot stock.
6. Now slowly stir the yogurt mixture into the hot stock.
7. Gently simmer for a further 5 to 10 minutes and remove from the heat.
8. Serve in a deep bowl accompanied by the rice.

paprikas csirke

CHICKEN PAPRIKA WITH YOGURT

This is a paprika dish from Hungary, flavored with the magnificent peppers of the region. The sauce is traditionally made with a mixture of cream and sour cream, but yogurt is an excellent substitute. It is usually accompanied by a bowl of small pasta shells.

1 chicken (about 3 lb/1½ kg),
  cut into 6 pieces
2 oz (50 g) lard
1 onion, finely chopped
2 tablespoons paprika
2 teaspoons salt
1 green pepper, cut into strips

3 tomatoes, blanched, peeled,
  seeded, and chopped
gnerous ½ cup (150 ml)
  chicken stock
1¼ cups (300 ml) yogurt, stabilized
  with 1 egg or 1 tablespoon all-
  purpose flour (see p. 17)

1. Wash and dry the chicken pieces.
2. In a large, heavy-based saucepan, melt the lard.
3. Add the chicken pieces and fry on both sides until golden brown, then place on a plate.
4. Add the onion to the remaining lard, cover, and cook very gently for about 20 minutes until soft and golden.
5. Stir in the paprika, salt, green pepper, and chopped tomatoes.
6. Return the chicken pieces to the pot and pour in the stock.
7. Turn the chicken pieces to ensure they are coated with the vegetables and liquid. They should be at least half covered with liquid; if not, add a little more.
8. Cover and simmer gently for ¾ to 1 hour until the chicken is tender.
9. Transfer the chicken to a serving dish and keep warm.
10. Pour the stabilized yogurt into a bowl and stir in 3 to 4 tablespoons of the paprika sauce.
11. Stir the yogurt mixture into the casserole, heat through, taste and adjust seasoning if necessary.
12. Pour the sauce over the chicken pieces and serve immediately.

dajaj mahshi

STUFFED CHICKEN MARINATED IN YOGURT

This dish is popular in one form or another throughout Turkey, Syria, Lebanon, Armenia, and Jordan. Ideal with fresh salads, yogurt, and a drink of *tan*.

1 roasting chicken (about 3–4 lb/ 1½–2 kg, with giblets)
4 tablespoons (2 oz/50 g) butter
1 small onion, finely chopped
1 tablespoon raisins
4 teaspoons salt
1 teaspoon black pepper

2 tablespoons pine nuts or slivered almonds
6 oz (175 g) rice, washed thoroughly
½ cinnamon stick
2 tablespoons (1 oz/25 g) butter, melted
2 tablespoons chopped parsley
1¼ cups (300 ml) yogurt

1. Remove giblets from the chicken, wash the liver and heart, and chop finely.
2. Melt the butter in a saucepan, add the onion, and sauté until golden brown.
3. Add the chopped giblets and pine nuts or almonds and cook for 2 to 3 minutes.
4. Stir in the rice and cook for about 5 minutes, turning frequently so that all the grains are coated with butter.
5. Add 2 cups (450 ml) water, the raisins, 2 teaspoons of the salt, ½ teaspoon of the black pepper, and the cinnamon stick.
6. Bring to a boil, lower the heat, and simmer until the liquid has been completely absorbed.
7. Remove from the heat, discard the cinnamon stick, and stir in the melted butter and parsley.
8. Wash the chicken and pat dry with paper towels.
9. Fill the cavity with the rice stuffing. If there is any remaining, set it aside to serve later with the chicken.
10. Tie the cavity closed.
11. Mix the remaining salt and black pepper with the yogurt.
12. Place the chicken in a bowl, pour the yogurt over the top, and rub it into the chicken, making sure that all parts are well coated.

13. Cover and leave in the refrigerator overnight.
14. Preheat the oven to 350°F (180°C) and roast, covered, for about 2½ hours until very tender and golden brown. Remove the lid for the last 30 minutes.
15. Transfer the chicken to a serving dish and spoon the stuffing into a separate dish.

murgi dahi

CHICKEN IN A YOGURT-CURRY SAUCE

Let me be honest and say that this is my favorite dish from the Indian subcontinent. Serve with bread or a rice pilaf.

8 chicken pieces, skinned
1¼ cups (300 ml) yogurt
1 onion, roughly chopped
3 garlic cloves
2 green chilis
1½ in (4 cm) piece fresh ginger, peeled and chopped
1 red or green pepper, seeded and coarsely chopped

1 teaspoon cumin seeds
1 teaspoon paprika
1 teaspoon salt
3 tablespoons (1½ oz/40 g) ghee or butter
2 tablespoons finely chopped cilantro
juice of ¼ lemon
fresh cilantro or mint leaves

1. Prick the chicken pieces all over with a fork, place in a bowl, and set aside.
2. In a blender, mix the yogurt, onion, garlic, chilis, ginger, cumin seeds, pepper, paprika, and salt together until smooth.
3. Pour this marinade over the chicken pieces and use your fingers to rub it in well.
4. Cover the bowl and set aside for 4 hours.
5. Put the chicken pieces and marinade into a large saucepan.
6. Bring to a boil over a moderate heat; when it has been bubbling for about 2 minutes, lower the heat and cook, stirring frequently, for 35 to 40 minutes or until the chicken is tender and the sauce is very thick.
7. Remove the pan from the heat.
8. Melt the butter in a large frying pan and add the chicken pieces.
9. Reduce the heat and fry the chicken pieces very gently, for 3 minutes, turning them frequently so that they are well coated in butter.
10. Spoon the sauce and the scrapings left in the saucepan over the chicken.
11. Sprinkle the chopped cilantro and lemon juice over the chicken, cover, and cook for a further 5 minutes.
12. Spoon the chicken and sauce onto a preheated dish and serve immediately, garnished with the cilantro or mint.

pecena divlja plorka

ROAST DUCK (OR GOOSE) WITH YOGURT SAUCE

This recipe normally calls for wild duck, but this is not readily available and so I suggest substituting ordinary duck or goose.

2 tablespoons (1 oz/25 g) butter

2 onions, sliced

1 duck or goose (about 5 lb/2½ kg), cleaned, washed, and dried

¼ cup oil

juice of 1 lemon

1 teaspoon salt

4–5 strips bacon

1 teaspoon cumin

1 bay leaf

salt and pepper to taste

2½ cups (600 ml) yogurt, stabilized with 1 egg (see p. 17)

1. Preheat the oven to 350°F (180°C).
2. Melt the butter in a saucepan and sauté the onions until soft.
3. Meanwhile, prick the skin of the bird in several places, then mix the oil, lemon juice, and salt together and rub the mixture into the skin.
4. Place the bacon strips over the breast of the bird.
5. When the onions are tender, add 1¼ cups (300 ml) water, cumin, bay leaf, salt, and pepper to taste, and bring to a boil.
6. Pour the mixture into the roasting pan and then place the bird in the center.
7. Roast for about 2 hours or until tender. Baste frequently with the sauce in the pan.
8. When cooked, remove the bird, carve, and keep the meat warm while you complete the sauce.
9. Add the yogurt to the sauce and heat through but do not boil.
10. Strain the sauce and pour it over the bird.
11. Serve immediately.

fish

yogurtlu uskumru dolmasi

MACKEREL STUFFED WITH PINE KERNELS AND CURRANTS

This is a slight variation on the great Turkish classic, *uskumru dolmasi*—stuffed mackerel. Traditionalists may object, but I do think the yogurt adds a subtle flavor to what is already a great dish.

4 whole mackerel, about 12 oz
  (350 g) each
salt
5 tablespoons olive oil

STUFFING
1 onion, finely chopped
2 oz (50 g) pine nuts
1 oz (25 g) fresh breadcrumbs
½ teaspoon coriander seeds
½ teaspoon ground cinnamon
black pepper to taste

3 tablespoons finely chopped
  parsley
2 oz (50 g) currants, soaked
  for 1 hour in warm water
3 tablespoons fresh dill
  or 3 teaspoons dried dill

4 tomatoes, sliced
1¼ cups (300 ml) yogurt,
  stabilized with 1 tablespoon
  all-purpose flour (see p. 17)
lemon wedges, to garnish

1. First prepare the fish for stuffing:
   a. Cut off the fins with scissors.
   b. Break the backbone at the base of the tail by bending the tail sharply
      forward over the body.
   c. Roll the fish backward and forward under the palms of your hands
      on a flat surface for a few minutes to loosen the backbone.
   d. Turn the fish over on to its back and cut down through the throat just
      behind the gills, leaving the head attached by a piece of skin about
      ½ in (1 cm) wide.

e. Scoop out and discard the entrails.

f. Wash the fish inside and out.

g. Hold the body tightly with one hand and with the other pull out the backbone.

h. Starting from the tail, gently press the fish with your thumbs to push out as much of the flesh as possible, being careful to keep the skin intact and the head attached so that the fish can be easily reassembled.

2. Place the fish shells in a large pan, sprinkle with salt, completely cover with cold water, and set aside for 30 minutes.

3. Place fish flesh in sieve, wash under cold running water, drain, pat dry with paper towels, and set aside.

4. Make the stuffing: heat ¼ cup of olive oil in a large pan.

5. Add the onion and sauté until soft.

6. Stir in the pine nuts and cook until lightly browned.

7. Add the fish flesh, breadcrumbs, coriander, cinnamon, 1 teaspoon of salt, and black pepper to taste.

8. Stir frequently and cook for 5 minutes.

9. Remove from the heat, stir in the parsley, currants, and dill, and set aside to cool.

10. Preheat oven to 400°F (200°C).

11. Brush the bottom and sides of a large, shallow ovenproof dish with 1 tablespoon of oil.

12. Wash the fish shells under cold running water and pat dry, inside and out, with paper towels.

13. Put a quarter of the stuffing into each fish.

14. Close the openings with needle and thread or small skewers.

15. Arrange the mackerel side by side in the dish.

16. Arrange the tomato slices along the length of each fish.

17. Blend a generous ½ cup (150 ml) water with the stabilized yogurt and pour into the dish.

18. Heat the dish on top of the stove until the sauce is about to boil and then transfer to the oven.

19. Bake for about 30 minutes or until the fish feels firm to the touch.

20. Serve immediately, garnished with the lemon wedges.

rascian carp

CARP WITH POTATOES AND YOGURT

This is an adaptation of a famous Hungarian recipe. Accompany with a simple cucumber and tomato salad.

1 whole carp, 5–6 lb (2½–3 kg)
1 teaspoon salt
1 teaspoon paprika
4 oz (100 g) Canadian bacon,
    cut into 2–3 in (5-8 cm) strips
2 lb (1 kg) potatoes
1 onion, sliced

2 green peppers, thinly sliced
3 large tomatoes, sliced
6 tablespoons (3 oz/75 g) butter,
    melted
2 cups (450 ml) yogurt, stabilized
    with 1 egg or 1 tablespoon all-
    purpose flour (see p. 17)

1. Preheat the oven to 350°F (180°C).
2. Scale, remove any entrails, and wash the fish under cold running water.
3. Using a sharp knife, split the fish into two and then cut into ½ lb (250 g) pieces and score them.
4. Sprinkle with the salt and paprika.
5. Put the thin slices of bacon into the incisions.
6. Meanwhile, peel, wash, and cut the potatoes into thick slices.
7. Parboil the potatoes in slightly-salted water for 5 minutes.
8. Now butter a large ovenproof dish and cover the bottom with the potatoes.
9. Put the fish into the dish and cover with sliced onion, paprikas or green peppers, and tomatoes.
10. Baste with the melted butter and put the dish into the oven.
11. When half cooked—after about 20 minutes—remove the dish from the oven and pour the stabilized yogurt over the fish. Return to the oven and continue cooking until both the fish and the potatoes are ready.

fish

maremkhodov tzook

TROUT WITH YOGURT AND MARJORAM

I was given this recipe by a friend who hails from Kurdistan. It is simple to make, attractive to look at, and has a subtle creamy flavor. Instead of trout you can use red or grey mullet.

Kaymak is the thick cream popular in the Middle East that is usually made from sheep's milk. Use heavy cream or, if you can get it, clotted cream.

Garnish with scallions and fresh tarragon leaves and serve with sweet boiled potatoes or sautéed potatoes.

4 whole trout (see method)
2 tablespoons (1 oz/25 g) ghee
   or butter, melted
1 tablespoon dried sweet marjoram
1 teaspoon salt
½ teaspoon black pepper
generous ½ cup (150 ml) yogurt

generous ½ cup (150 ml) *kaymak*,
   heavy cream, or clotted cream
1 tablespoon all-purpose flour
2 limes or lemons, cut into wedges,
   to garnish
scallions and fresh tarragon, to
   garnish

1. Ask your fishmonger to remove the entrails and clean out the fish.
2. Preheat the oven to 350°F (180°C).
3. Wash the fish under cold running water and dry with paper towels.
4. Place the fish side by side in a lightly buttered baking dish.
5. Brush the melted ghee or butter over the fish and then sprinkle with the marjoram, salt, and pepper.
6. Mix the yogurt and cream together in a bowl and then stir in the flour.
7. Pour this mixture over the fish and bake for 30 to 45 minutes or until the fish are well cooked.
8. Serve garnished with the lime or lemon wedges, scallions, and tarragon.

shrimp pathia

CURRIED SHRIMP IN YOGURT

This popular Indian dish makes use of shrimp and a yogurt-based curry sauce. It has a delicate flavor and is excellent on a bed of boiled rice or eaten with *naan* or *parathas*.

8 tablespoons (4 oz/100 g) ghee or butter

2 medium onions, finely chopped

3 oz (75 g) coarse shredded coconut

1 teaspoon chili powder

1 teaspoon paprika

2 in (5 cm) cinnamon stick

3 bay leaves

1½ teaspoons *garam masala*

1 tablespoon fenugreek

1 teaspoon ground ginger

2 tablespoons tomato paste

2 cups (450 ml) stabilized yogurt (see p. 17)

1 lb (½ kg) frozen shrimp, thawed, or use fresh shrimp

1. In a large saucepan, melt the ghee or butter and fry the onions until golden brown.
2. Add the coconut and cook until light brown.
3. Add the chili powder, paprika, cinnamon, bay leaves, *garam masala*, fenugreek, and ginger, and stir well.
4. Stir in the tomato paste and yogurt.
5. Bring to a boil and immediately lower the heat.
6. Add the shrimp and stir well.
7. Cover the pan and simmer slowly, stirring frequently to prevent sticking, for 30 minutes or until the shrimp are well cooked and the sauce is thick.

som baligi

SALMON WITH YOGURT

This is an adaptation of a popular Turkish dish. Salmon is highly prized among the Turks and is reserved for special occasions. The dish is found in most good Istanbul and Ismir restaurants.

4 salmon steaks

1 small carrot, grated

1 small onion, chopped

1 stick celery, chopped

2 bay leaves

1 garlic clove, chopped

2 cloves

4 peppercorns

8 oz (250 g) cooked spinach, chopped

2 tablespoons all-purpose flour

1¼ cups (300 ml) yogurt

1½ teaspoons salt

½ teaspoon nutmeg

1 oz (25 g) breadcrumbs

2 oz (50 g) halloumi or
Parmesan cheese, grated

1. Place the salmon steaks in a large, deep saucepan and add sufficient boiling water to cover.
2. Add the carrot, onion, celery, bay leaves, garlic, cloves, and peppercorns.
3. Simmer until the fish can easily be separated from the bone.
4. Using a slotted spoon, tranfer the fish steaks to a plate and keep hot.
5. Raise the heat and boil vigorously until the stock has been reduced to 2 to 2½ cups (450–600 ml) and then strain, retaining the stock and discarding the vegetables.
6. Meanwhile, prepare the spinach and keep it warm.
7. Put the flour into a small bowl, add 3–4 tablespoons of the hot stock, and stir until smooth.
8. Preheat the broiler.
9. Add the flour mixture to the remaining stock and heat through, stirring constantly until the sauce thickens. Simmer very gently for 5 to 10 minutes.
10. Remove the sauce from the heat and stir in the yogurt, salt, and nutmeg.
11. Arrange the spinach on a ovenproof serving dish and arrange the fish steaks on it.
12. Pour the sauce over the top.
13. Sprinkle with the breadcrumbs and cheese and place under a broiler for 3 to 5 minutes until golden brown.
14. Serve immediately.

fish curry

The finest fish dishes on the Indian subcontinent originate in Bangladesh, which has an abundance of fish of all kinds.

1 lb (½ kg) fish, e.g. tuna, bonito, or halibut
1 teaspoon turmeric
1 teaspoon salt
½ teaspoon grated ginger
2 fresh green chili peppers
2 fresh red chili peppers or 2 teaspoons chili powder

1¼ cups (300 ml) stabilized yogurt (see p. 17)
¼ cup mustard oil or vegetable oil
4 tablespoons (2 oz/50 g) ghee or butter
1 onion, finely chopped
2 bay leaves
1½ teaspoons curry powder

1. Clean, scale, and wash the fish. Cut into ten to twelve pieces.
2. Mix the turmeric, salt, and grated ginger together.
3. Rub the mixture into the fish.
4. Seed the chilis and finely slice them.
5. Pour the yogurt into a bowl and stir in the chilis or chili powder.
6. Meanwhile, heat the mustard or vegetable oil in a large saucepan, add the ghee or butter and onion, and sauté until soft and lightly browned.
7. Add the yogurt mixture, bay leaves, and curry powder, stir and cook gently for a few minutes.
8. Add the fish pieces and turn until they are well coated and then simmer for about 20 minutes or until the fish flakes easily and the sauce has thickened.
9. Serve on a bed of saffron rice pilaf.

madznov ishkan

STUFFED TROUT WITH ALMOND AND YOGURT SAUCE

This is traditionally made with the trout called *ishkan*—"prince of trout"—endemic to Lake Sevan in Armenia, where they are now protected from commercial fishing. Brown or rainbow trout are suitable substitutes.

4 whole trout
cooking oil or butter

STUFFING
¼ lb (100 g) ground almonds
juice of 2 lemons
about ½ cup (150 ml) yogurt
1 teaspoon salt
1 teaspoon black pepper
1 teaspoon cumin

SAUCE
¼ lb (100 g) ground almonds
1 cup dry white wine
about ½ cup (150 ml) yogurt,
  stabilized (see p. 17)
salt and black pepper to taste
a few thin slices green pepper

GARNISH
lemon wedges

1. Have your fishmonger clean the fish, but do not have the heads or tails removed.
2. Preheat the oven to 400°F (200°C).
3. In a bowl, combine and mix the stuffing ingredients.
4. If needed, add more yogurt to produce a thick paste.
5. Divide the mixture into four and stuff the cavity of each trout.
6. Heat the butter or oil in a large baking dish.
7. Place the fish in the dish, brush with a little oil, and bake for 20 to 30 minutes.
8. Meanwhile, prepare the sauce: in a small saucepan, mix the almonds with the wine and yogurt.
9. Season with the salt and pepper.
10. Add sufficient water to make the consistency that you prefer.
11. Bring to a boil and then simmer gently for about 10 minutes.
12. Just before serving, add the green pepper. Do not cook for more than a minute or two or it will lose its crispness and color.
13. When the fish are cooked, arrange them on a large dish with the lemon wedges and serve with the sauce.

plaice casserole

This is a simple, relatively inexpensive dish to prepare. I have chosen plaice because I like its delicate taste, but there is no reason why you should not use flounder, brill, or turbot. Accompany it with a cooked vegetable of your choice and boiled or roast potatoes.

1 whole plaice (about 1–1½ lb/
  ½–¾ kg), or any other flat fish
butter, for greasing
1¼ cups (300 ml) yogurt
1 egg yolk, well beaten
3 tablespoons dry white wine
1½ tablespoons lemon juice

½ teaspoon dried oregano
1 teaspoon salt
a pinch of paprika
2–3 bay leaves
2 oz (50 g) breadcrumbs
2 tablespoons finely chopped
  parsley

1. Ask your fishmonger to clean out the fish, leaving it intact. Otherwise, you can do it yourself: make a semicircular slit just behind the head on the dark skin side. The cavity that opens here contains the entrails. Scrape these out, wash the fish thoroughly, and cut off the fins.
2. Preheat the oven to 375°F (190°C).
3. Arrange the fish in a buttered baking dish.
4. Pour the yogurt into a bowl, add the egg yolk, wine, lemon juice, oregano, salt, and paprika, and beat lightly.
5. Pour this mixture over the fish and add the bay leaves.
6. Sprinkle the breadcrumbs over the top and bake for 50 minutes or so.
7. Just before serving, garnish with the parsley.

tirana fish stew

ALBANIAN FISH STEW

Another Balkan specialty, this time from Albania. Serve on a bed of rice pilaf or boiled noodles.

3 tablespoons olive oil
1 onion, thinly sliced
1 garlic clove, finely chopped
2 tablespoons tomato paste
1 cup dry white wine
6 potatoes, peeled and thinly sliced
2 bay leaves
1 teaspoon salt
½ teaspoon black pepper

¼ teaspoon dried basil
¼ teaspoon cayenne pepper
1½ lb (750 g) white fish e.g. halibut
    or cod, cut into 1–1½ in (3–4 cm)
    pieces
1¼ cups (300 ml) yogurt, stabilized
    with 1 egg (see p. 17)
2 tablespoons finely chopped
    parsley

1. Heat the oil in a large saucepan and sauté the onion and garlic until soft and translucent.
2. Add the tomato paste and stir well.
3. Add 2½ cups (600 ml) water, along with the wine, potatoes, bay leaves, salt, black pepper, basil, and cayenne pepper, and mix well.
4. Cover the pan and cook on medium heat for 10 to 12 minutes.
5. Add the fish pieces and cook for a further 15 to 20 minutes or until the potatoes and fish are tender.
6. Mix in the yogurt and parsley and heat through but do not boil.
7. Serve immediately.

bulgarian fish with yogurt

This is a typically Balkan dish, flavored with paprika, grated cheese, mushrooms, oregano, and yogurt. It is popular throughout Eastern Europe; the Romanians and Hungarians use sour cream, while the Bulgarians prefer yogurt.

2 lb (1 kg) halibut
flour, for dusting
salt and pepper
4 tablespoons (2 oz/50 g) butter,
    melted
2 hard-boiled eggs,
    shelled and sliced
2 oz (50 g) mushrooms, washed,

dried, and thinly sliced
2 tablespoons paprika
2 oz (50 g) grated cheese e.g.
    Parmesan, Cheddar, or
    halloumi—I prefer the latter
1¼ cups (300 ml) yogurt,
    stabilized with 1 tablespoon
    all-purpose flour (see p. 17)

1. Preheat the oven to 350°F (180°C).
2. Wash the fish, dry thoroughly, and cut into 2 in (5 cm) pieces, discarding the bones.
3. Dust with flour and sprinkle with salt and pepper.
4. Pour the butter into a baking dish and arrange the fish in the dish.
5. Arrange the egg slices and mushrooms over the fish.
6. Sprinkle with the paprika.
7. Mix the cheese and yogurt and spoon over the fish, egg, and mushrooms.
8. Bake in the center of the oven for about 30 minutes or until the fish flakes easily with a fork.
9. Serve, accompanied by a green salad and boiled potatoes.

tzavarov letzonadze tzook

FISH STUFFED WITH BULGAR

This Caucasian dish is traditionally made with bream, but any white fish will do. It is usually stuffed with kasha (buckwheat groats), but I think *tzavar* (bulgar) is far better. The Circassians and Georgians use sour cream instead of yogurt.

2–3 lb (1–1½ kg) whole white fish, e.g. bream, halibut, cod, etc.

6 tablespoons (3 oz/75 g) butter

2 onions, finely chopped

12 oz (350 g) coarse bulgar

3 hard-boiled eggs, shelled and coarsely chopped

2 tablespoons finely chopped parsley

2 tablespoons fresh dill or 2 teaspoons dried dill

1 teaspoon salt

½ teaspoon black pepper

1¼ cups (300 ml) yogurt, stabilized with 1 tablespoon all-purpose flour (see p. 17)

1 teaspoon sumac

1. Remove the entrails and wash the fish under cold running water; dry thoroughly with paper towels.
2. Preheat the oven to 400°F (200°C).
3. In a large saucepan, melt 2 oz (50 g) of the butter and sauté the onions until soft.
4. Add the bulgar, chopped eggs, parsley, dill, salt, and pepper. Mix thoroughly and cook gently for 4 to 5 minutes.
5. Sprinkle the cavity of the fish with a little salt and spoon the bulgar mixture into the cavity. Do not press too hard as the bulgar will expand during cooking.
6. Arrange the fish in a large buttered baking dish.
7. Dot little knobs of the remaining butter over the fish.
8. Bake in the center of the oven for 10 to 15 minutes, or until the fish is almost tender.
9. Remove the baking dish, pour the yogurt over the fish, and return it to the center of the oven.
10. Cook for a further 5 to 8 minutes.
11. Remove from the oven and sprinkle with the sumac.
12. Serve with *lavash* or pita bread and a bowl of fresh herbs and vegetables such as sliced cucumbers and tomatoes.

caucasian hake

This is a classic dish of the Caucasus and I understand that a very similar dish is extremely popular in the Balkans. It is a tasty fish casserole traditionally served with a bowl of fresh herbs like tarragon, parsley, chives, and scallions. Although there are potatoes in the dish I find that a few extra sautéed potatoes make an ideal accompaniment.

4 fish steaks—preferably hake, but halibut or cod will do
1 lb (½ kg) potatoes, peeled and cut into ¼ in (½ cm) rounds
1 onion, thinly sliced
4 tablespoons (2 oz/50 g) butter
3 tomatoes, thinly sliced

1 teaspoon salt
1 tablespoon sumac
2 cups (450 ml) yogurt
1 tablespoon flour
2 teaspoons paprika

1. Wash the steaks under cold running water and pat dry with paper towels.
2. Lightly butter a large ovenproof dish and preheat oven to 325°F (160°C).
3. Arrange the slices of potato and onion in the dish and dot with the butter.
4. Arrange the slices of tomato over the top and sprinkle with the salt and sumac.
5. Cover and cook in the oven for 30 to 40 minutes.
6. Remove from the oven and place the fish steaks on top of the vegetables.
7. Mix the yogurt, flour, and paprika together with 2 or 3 tablespoons of the hot sauce and pour over the fish.
8. Cover, return to the oven, and cook for a further 45 minutes or until the fish is well cooked.
9. Serve immediately.

machchi kebab

From India, this skewered fish kebab is marinated in all the regional spices. Traditionally cooked in a *tandoor*, it is also excellent when cooked on the grill or, for convenience, under the broiler, though of course the flavor will not be quite the same. Serve with *chapatis* or pita bread and an accompaniment of thinly sliced onions, green chilis, and mint leaves dressed with lime juice.

2 lb (1 kg) fish, e.g. snapper, hake, or haddock, filleted

MARINADE
2 teaspoons fresh ginger, finely chopped
2 garlic cloves, finely chopped
2 teaspoons salt
1 teaspoon *garam masala*
juice of 2 lemons
1¼ cups (300 ml) yogurt
1 teaspoon chili powder
3 teaspoons ground coriander
2 tablespoons all-purpose flour

1. Wash the fish and dry with paper towels.
2. Cut the fish into 1 in (3 cm) pieces.
3. Put all the marinade ingredients together in a large bowl and mix together thoroughly.
4. Add the fish cubes, toss them in the marinade, and leave for 30 minutes at room temperature or for 1 hour, covered, in the refrigerator.
5. Thread the fish cubes on to skewers and, watching carefully so they don't overcook, broil or grill for about 10 minutes, turning once or twice.
6. Remove from the grill or oven and serve immediately.

barz tzook

FISH WITH WALNUTS

The translation of this name is "simple fish" and that is just what it is—fish with yogurt and herbs. It is popular throughout the Middle East, but especially in the Caucasus and northern Iran, where great use is made of fresh herbs. The crumbly topping makes this a very attractive dish.

4 white fish steaks, e.g. cod, halibut, or swordfish (about 2 lb/1 kg)
1 teaspoon salt
½ teaspoon black pepper
1¼ cups (300 ml) yogurt, stabilized with 1 tablespoon all-purpose flour (see p. 17)
juice of 1 lemon

3–4 scallions, finely chopped
2 oz (50 g) breadcrumbs
2 oz (50 g) chopped walnuts
2 tablespoons (1 oz/25 g) butter, melted
2 tablespoons finely chopped parsley
1 tablespoon finely chopped fresh basil or 1 teaspoon dried basil

1. Preheat the oven to 350°F (180°C).
2. Wash the fish steaks and pat them dry on paper towels.
3. Sprinkle both sides of the fish with salt and pepper to taste.
4. Lightly butter a large shallow baking dish and arrange the fish steaks in the bottom.
5. Mix the yogurt with the lemon juice and the chopped scallions and spoon over the fish.
6. Now mix the breadcrumbs and the walnuts into the melted butter, together with the parsley and basil.
7. Spread this mixture over the fish and bake for 30 to 40 minutes or until the fish steaks flake easily with a fork.
8. This dish is traditionally served with individual side dishes of herbs, such as scallions, radishes, dill, tarragon, etc.

accompaniments

plain rice pilaf

When cooking rice, volume is more important than weight and the general rule is as follows: for the first cup of rice (6 oz, 175 g) use 2 cups of liquid (475 ml) and for every further cup of rice use 1½ cups of liquid (350 ml). This is the basic Middle Eastern method.

4 tablespoons (2 oz/50 g) butter
  or ghee
9 oz (250 g) long-grain rice, washed
  thoroughly under cold water
  and drained

1 teaspoon salt
2½ cups (600 ml) boiling water
  or stock

1. Melt the butter or ghee in a saucepan.
2. Add the rice and fry for 2 to 3 minutes, stirring frequently.
3. Stir in the salt and boiling stock or water.
4. Allow the mixture to boil vigorously for about 3 minutes and then cover, lower the heat, and simmer for 15 to 20 minutes or until the liquid has been absorbed.
5. The grains should be tender and separate and there should be small holes in the surface of the pilaf.
6. Turn off the heat, remove the lid, cover the saucepan with a clean dish towel, replace the lid, and leave to "rest" for 10 to 15 minutes.
7. Gently fluff up the rice with a fork, taking care not to break the grains, and serve.

bulgar pilavi

CRACKED WHEAT PILAF

A particular favorite of Armenians and Turks, bulgar has, in recent years, appeared in the West. Bulgar can be bought from many Middle Eastern and health food stores. When purchasing it to make a pilaf make sure that you buy the coarse bulgar. It makes an excellent pilaf and is, perhaps, the grain that goes best with yogurt. It has a strong, earthy flavor and color.

9 oz (250 g) coarse bulgar

4 tablespoons (2 oz/50 g) butter
  or ghee

1 oz (25 g) vermicelli, broken
  into 1 in (2.5 cm) pieces

2 cups (450 ml) stock or water,
  boiling

1 teaspoon salt

½ teaspoon black pepper

1. Put the bulgar into a bowl or fine sieve and wash several times until the water runs clear. Leave to drain.
2. Melt the butter or ghee in a saucepan.
3. Add the vermicelli and fry until golden, stirring constantly.
4. Add the bulgar and fry for a further 2 or 3 minutes, stirring frequently.
5. Add the boiling stock or water, salt and pepper, and stir well.
6. Bring to a boil and boil vigorously for 3 minutes.
7. Lower the heat and simmer for 8 to 10 minutes or until the water has been absorbed.
8. Turn off the heat, cover the pan with a clean dish towel, fit a lid over the top, and leave to "rest" for 10 to 15 minutes before serving.

khubz

Perhaps the most popular Middle Eastern bread, pita is Syrian by origin and was known by the ancient Assyrians and Babylonians who filled its pocket with vegetables or cooked meats—as is still the custom today.

You can purchase pita bread from most grocery stores, but if you wish to bake your own then try this recipe (see picture opposite).

MAKES EIGHT

½ oz (15 g) fresh yeast or 2¼ teaspoons (¼ oz/8g) active dry yeast

1 teaspoon sugar

3½ cups (1 lb/450 g) all-purpose flour

½ teaspoon salt

1 tablespoon oil (optional)

1. Place the yeast and sugar in a small bowl, dissolve in a few tablespoons warm water, and set aside in a warm place for about 10 minutes or until it begins to froth.
2. Sift the flour and salt into a large bowl.
3. Make a well in the center and pour in the yeast mixture.
4. Add enough warm water (about 1¼ cups/300 ml) to make a firm, but not hard, dough.
5. Knead on a floured work surface for 10 to 15 minutes or until the dough is soft and elastic. If you knead in a tablespoon of oil it will make a softer dough.
6. Wash and dry the mixing bowl and lightly oil it.
7. Roll the dough around the bowl until its surface is greased all over— this will prevent the dough going crusty and cracking as it rises.
8. Cover the dough with a damp cloth and set aside in a warm place for at least 2 hours until the dough has doubled in size.
9. Transfer the dough to the work surface, punch down, and knead for a few minutes.
10. Divide the mixture into eight pieces.
11. Roll them between your palms until they are round and smooth.

12. Lightly flour the work surface and flatten each ball with the palm of your hand or a rolling pin until it is about ¼ in (½ cm) thick and is as even and circular as possible.

13. Dust the tops with flour and cover with a floured cloth.

14. Preheat the oven to 450–475°F (230–240°C), putting in two large oiled baking sheets halfway through the heating period.

15. Leave the dough rounds to rise in a warm place for a further 20 to 30 minutes.

16. When the oven is ready, slide the rounds on to the hot baking sheets, damping the tops of the rounds of dough to prevent them browning, and bake for 10 minutes, without opening the oven door.

17. Once this time has passed, it is safe to open the door to see if the pitas have puffed up.

18. Slide them on to wire racks as soon as you remove them from the oven.

19. They should be soft and white with a pouch inside.

lavash

THIN CRISPY BREAD

This is the bread of Armenia similar to *naan*. It often measures up to 2 ft (60 cm) in diameter and is only ⅛ in (3mm) thick. Baked in a *tonir* (*tandoor*), it is always made in large quantities and then stacked and stored for winter use.

Lavash goes well with many dishes, but is particularly good with kebabs, roasts, and salads.

½ oz (15 g) fresh yeast or
  2¼ teaspoons (¼ oz/8 g) active
  dry yeast

1 teaspoon sugar
5½ cup (1½ lb/680 g) all-purpose flour
1 teaspoon salt

1. Place the yeast in a small bowl with the sugar, dissolve in 1¼ cups (300 ml) warm water, and set aside for about 10 minutes in a warm place until the mixture begins to froth.
2. Sift the flour and salt into a large bowl.
3. Make a well in the center and slowly work in the yeast mixture and enough warm water to make a stiff dough.
4. Knead on a floured surface for about 10 minutes until the dough is smooth and elastic.
5. Place the ball of dough in a clean bowl, cover with a cloth, and leave in a warm place for about 2 to 3 hours or until it has doubled in size.
6. Transfer the dough to a floured surface, punch it down, and knead again for a few minutes.
7. Return to the bowl, cover, and leave for a further 30 minutes.
8. Flour the work surface again.
9. Divide the dough into apple-sized balls. This amount of dough should make twelve to fifteen.
10. Using a long rolling pin, roll out each ball into a thin sheet about 8–10 inches (20–25 cm) in diameter, sprinkling the work surface with flour now and again to prevent sticking
11. Adjust the bottom shelf of your oven so that it is as low as possible. Line a baking sheet with foil and place it on the bottom shelf. Preheat the oven to 400°F (200°C).
12. Place a sheet of dough on the foil and bake for about 3 minutes.
13. Remove the cooked *lavash* and cover with a dish towel while you bake the remaining *lavash* in the same way.
14. Serve immediately.
15. If the *lavash* are not to be used at once, let them cool fully. Fold and wrap them in a dish towel, seal in a plastic bag, and freeze. When ready to serve, defrost them. Sprinkle them lightly with water, wrap in a dish towel, and leave for 10 minutes to absorb the moisture and to soften.

chapati

Thin, round, unleavened bread often sold in Indian restaurants. Similar to the Arab *shapatieh*, this bread is an ideal accompaniment for most meat dishes, but particularly kebabs and stews. Very simple to prepare, the recipe below is from northern India. The whole-wheat flour gives the bread an earthy color and texture.

MAKES EIGHT

2 cups (8 oz/225 g) whole-wheat flour
½ teaspoon salt

4 tablespoons (2 oz/50 g) butter
 or vegetable oil
1 tablespoon melted clarified butter

1. Sift the flour and salt into a large mixing bowl.
2. Add the butter or oil and rub it into the flour until the mixture resembles fine breadcrumbs.
3. Make a well in the center and pour in ⅓ cup (90 ml) water.
4. Draw the flour into the water with your fingers and mix well, gradually adding another ¼ cup (60 ml) water.
5. Form the dough into a ball and place it on a floured work surface.
6. Knead for about 10 minutes or until it has become smooth and elastic.
7. Put the dough into a bowl, cover with a cloth, and leave to stand for 30 minutes at room temperature.
8. Divide the dough into eight portions and roll into balls between the palms of your hands.
9. On a floured surface, roll out each ball of dough into a thin round about 6 in (15 cm) across.
10. Meanwhile, heat a heavy-based frying pan or griddle. When it is hot, place a circle of dough in it.
11. When small blisters appear on the surface press the *chapati* to flatten it.
12. When the underside is pale golden turn it over and cook the remaining side in the same way.
13. Remove from the pan and brush on both sides with a little of the clarified butter.

14. Place on a plate and cover with another plate to keep it warm while you cook the remaining *chapatis* in the same way.
15. Serve warm.

naan

PUNJABI LEAVENED FLATBREAD

Traditionally this bread is cooked in a *tandoor*—a large clay oven—and it get its tear-drop shape from being stuck to the wall of the oven and stretching while it cooks. Serve it with kebabs and dishes from the Indian subcontinent.

MAKES EIGHT

1 teaspoon active dry yeast
generous ½ cup (150 ml) yogurt
3 teaspoons sugar
1 egg, beaten
4 tablespoons (2 oz/50 g) ghee
  or butter, melted

2 teaspoons salt
3 cups (12 oz/350 g) all-purpose flour
a little melted ghee or butter for
  glazing
2 tablespoons poppyseeds or
  sesame seeds (optional)

1. Put the yeast into a small bowl with a little lukewarm water and stir until dissolved.
2. Leave in a warm place.
3. Put the yogurt into a bowl and beat until smooth.
4. Add ½ cup (150 ml) lukewarm water, sugar, egg, melted ghee, and salt, and mix well.
5. When the yeast has begun to work and there is a froth on the surface, pour the yeast mixture into the bowl with the other liquid ingredients and stir.
6. Sift about 2 cups (8 oz/250 g) of the flour into a large mixing bowl, make a well in the center, and pour in the liquid mixture.
7. Stir and knead until you have a smooth batter.
8. Now slowly knead in the remaining flour until you have a soft dough.
9. Remove to a lightly floured surface and knead for 10 to 15 minutes until it is smooth and elastic. Dust with flour if it is a little sticky.
10. Form the dough into a ball, put into a large bowl, cover with a damp cloth, and set aside in a warm place for 2 to 3 hours.
11. Remove the dough from the bowl and knead for a few minutes to remove the air bubbles and to ensure a good rise and even texture.

12. Preheat oven to 450°F (230°C) and oil two large baking sheets.
13. Divide the dough into six to eight balls, depending on the size of bread wanted, and leave to rest for 10 minutes.
14. Pat the balls into 6–8 in (15–20 cm) circles, making them slightly thinner in the center and thicker around the rim.
15. Now pull one end outwards—like a large tear-drop.
16. Brush both sides with ghee and place two loaves on each oiled baking sheet.
17. If using, sprinkle the tops with the poppy seeds or sesame seeds.
18. Bake in the oven for about 10 minutes or until nicely puffed and golden brown.
19. Repeat with the remaining dough.
20. Serve immediately in order to appreciate the fragrance.

kela pach chadi

BANANAS IN SPICED YOGURT

From Hyderabad, India, these are usually served as an accompaniment to curry, but they are also very good with kebabs.

3 large ripe bananas
3 tablespoons freshly grated or
  dried shredded coconut
1¼ cups (300 ml) yogurt
2 tablespoons lemon juice
2 teaspoons sugar

½ teaspoon salt
⅛ teaspoon chili powder (optional)
1 teaspoon ghee or oil
1 teaspoon cumin seeds
½ teaspoon black mustard seeds

1. Peel and slice the bananas. There should be approximately 11 oz (300 g) of sliced banana.
2. If using dried shredded coconut, sprinkle 1 tablespoon hot water over it and mix until coconut is evenly moistened.
3. Season the yogurt with lemon juice, sugar, salt, and chili power, and stir in the bananas and coconut.
4. In a small saucepan, heat the ghee and fry the cumin and mustard seeds until the mustard seeds pop.
5. Pour this over the yogurt mixture and fold in.
6. Serve.

sauces, dressings & drinks

orga's yogurt dressing

This recipe is Irfan Orga's, from his book *Cooking with Yogurt*. It is an extremely versatile dressing that goes well with poultry and fish as well as salads.

1½ tablespoons sifted flour
½ teaspoon sugar
½ teaspoon salt
½ teaspoon dry mustard
¼ cup (60 ml) tarragon vinegar

2 egg yolks
generous ½ cup (150 ml) olive oil
¼ cup (75 ml) yogurt
2 tablespoons finely chopped chives

1. Into a saucepan put the flour, sugar, salt, dry mustard, vinegar, and ¾ cup (200 ml) water.
2. Cook over a low heat until the sauce thickens, stirring all the time. Bring to a boil for a minute or so and remove from the heat.
3. Beat in the egg yolks and continue beating.
4. Add the olive oil gradually.
5. Chill well, for at least 4 hours.
6. An hour before serving add the yogurt and chives. Beat for 1 minute.

horseradish sauce

An adaptation of the classic French version. Goes well with cold cuts, roasts, and kebabs.

1 tablespoon (½ oz/15 g) butter
1 tablespoon sifted flour
1 oz (25 g) grated horseradish
1¼ cups (300 ml) yogurt

2 tablespoons tarragon vinegar
½ teaspoon superfine sugar
1 teaspoon salt
½ teaspoon cayenne pepper

1. Melt the butter in a pan, add flour, and stir until smooth.
2. Add the horseradish and yogurt, stirring all the time.
3. Bring to a boil, lower the heat, and cook until thick and creamy.
4. Add the vinegar, sugar, salt, and cayenne and stir well.
5. Remove from heat and allow to cool. Refrigerate for 1 to 2 hours.
6. Serve cold.

tarçinli yogurt sos

CINNAMON YOGURT SAUCE

An Anatolian favorite.

1¼ cups (300 ml) yogurt
2 teaspoons sugar

1 teaspoon ground cinnamon

1. Pour the yogurt into a serving bowl, add the sugar, and mix well.
2. Sprinkle with cinnamon.
3. Serve as an accompaniment to meat dishes, grills, roasts, etc.

sughtorov madzoon

GARLIC YOGURT SAUCE

Yogurt and garlic go very well together and this recipe is by far the most popular throughout the Middle East. It can be served with virtually any dish, hot or cold.

1¼ cups (300 ml) yogurt
1 garlic clove, crushed
¼ teaspoon salt

½ teaspoon dried mint
1 scallion, finely chopped (optional)

1. Pour the yogurt into a bowl.
2. Mix the garlic and salt together, add to the yogurt, and mix well.
3. Sprinkle the top with dried mint and the onion if using it.
4. Serve with fried vegetables, lamb or beef dishes, etc.

yogurt salad dressing

Yogurt enlivens the flavor of this creamy mayonnaise-based salad dressing, which is particularly good with coleslaw, but can accompany any green salad.

2 egg yolks, at room temperature
½ teaspoon salt
⅛ teaspoon white pepper
¾ teaspoon dry mustard
1 cup (250 ml) olive oil, at room
  temperature

1 tablespoon white wine, vinegar,
  or lemon juice
¼ cup yogurt
1 teaspoon sugar
½ teaspoon salt
1 tablespoon grated onion
1 tablespoon finely chopped celery

1. To prepare the mayonnaise, place the egg yolks, salt, pepper, and mustard in a mixing bowl.

2. Using a wire whisk, beat until thoroughly blended.

3. Slowly add the oil, a few drops at a time, whisking constantly. Do not add the oil too quickly or the mayonnaise will curdle.

4. After the mayonnaise has thickened the oil may be added a little more rapidly.

5. Beat in a few drops of vinegar or lemon juice from time to time to prevent the mayonnaise becoming too thick.

6. When all the oil has been added, stir in the remaining vinegar or lemon juice.

7. Blend the mayonnaise with the yogurt, mixing well with a wooden spoon.

8. Add the remaining ingredients and beat for 1 minute.

9. Use immediately.

yogurt and herb mayonnaise

Excellent for chicken or poached fish, boiled eggs, and salads.

generous ½ cup (150 ml) yogurt

generous ½ cup (150 ml) mayonnaise

1 teaspoon Dijon mustard

1 tablespoon lemon juice

2 tablespoons chopped parsley

2 tablespoons chopped chives

2 tablespoons fresh tarragon, chopped

1. In a bowl whisk the yogurt and mayonnaise until well blended.

2. Add the mustard, lemon juice, and the herbs.

3. Mix well.

4. Serve.

avocado yogurt sauce

Serve as a sauce for shrimp or seafood cocktails. This recipe is from Israel.

1 avocado
1 tablespoon fresh lemon juice
¼ cup (60 ml) bottled chili sauce

1 teaspoon Worcestershire sauce
½ cup (120 ml) yogurt
salt and pepper to taste

1. Peel the avocado and cut in half.
2. Remove the pit and mash the flesh to a purée.
3. Add the lemon juice and mix well.
4. Add all the remaining ingredients and chill.

watercress yogurt dressing

A very tasty dressing for a seafood dish or a shrimp cocktail.

½ cup (120 ml) mayonnaise
¼ cup (60 ml) tomato paste
2 teaspoons fresh lemon juice
2 teaspoons prepared
  horseradish sauce

salt and pepper to taste
1 cup (250 ml) yogurt
1 large bunch watercress,
  washed and finely chopped

1. Mix together all the ingredients, except the watercress, and place in the refrigerator to chill.
2. Stir in the watercress just before serving.

madznov ganachi salsa

YOGURT HERB DRESSING

Serve with fish dishes.

1¼ cups (300 ml) yogurt
2 tablespoons finely chopped
  celery leaves
1 teaspoon chopped parsley
1 tablespoon chopped chives
1 tablespoon grated horseradish

1 tablespoon lemon juice
½ teaspoon paprika
½ teaspoon salt
1 garlic clove, crushed
1 teaspoon sumac

1. Beat the yogurt until creamy.
2. Stir in all remaining ingredients, except the sumac.
3. Taste and adjust seasoning if necessary.
4. Sprinkle the sumac on top.

yogurt fish sauce

A piquant sauce that goes well with hot or cold cooked fish.

generous ½ cup (150 ml) yogurt
generous ½ cup (150 ml)
  mayonnaise

1 teaspoon lemon juice
½ teaspoon cayenne pepper
1 tablespoon chopped parsley

1. In a bowl mix the yogurt and mayonnaise, and then add the lemon juice and
   cayenne pepper. Stir well.
2. Sprinkle chopped parsley on top and serve.

yogurt tartare sauce

Serve this sauce with fish.

generous ½ cup (150 ml) mayonnaise
generous ½ cup (150 ml) yogurt
2 tablespoons finely chopped
   green pepper
1 tablespoon finely chopped onion

2 tablespoons finely chopped
   sweet pickle
1 tablespoon finely chopped parsley
1 tablespoon capers
salt and pepper to taste

1. Mix all the ingredients together and chill.

sauce hollandaise with yogurt

An alternative to the well-known hollandaise. Serve hot or cold with fish or other lightly flavored dishes and with grilled or fried vegetables.

4 egg yolks, beaten
1 cup (250 ml) yogurt, stabilized
   with 1 egg or 1 tablespoon all-
   purpose flour (see p. 17)
6 tablespoons (3 oz/75 g) butter

salt and pepper to taste
1 teaspoon grated lemon rind or
   2 teaspoons tarragon vinegar
1 teaspoon lemon juice

1. Strain the beaten egg yolks into the top of a double boiler over boiling water.
2. Add the yogurt slowly and stir constantly until the mixture thickens.
3. Whisk the butter into the sauce, 2 tablespoons (1 oz/25 g) at a time, until it is smooth and glossy.
4. Add salt and pepper to taste, the lemon rind or tarragon vinegar, and lemon juice.
5. Remove from the heat immediately.

yogurt mustard sauce

I find this sauce excellent with fish and chicken dishes, but especially with cooked vegetables such as celery, leeks, and broccoli. The sumac gives the sauce color as well as flavor.

generous ½ cup (150 ml) yogurt
2 egg yolks
1 teaspoon lemon juice
½ teaspoon salt

¼ teaspoon black pepper
½ teaspoon fennel seeds
1 teaspoon sumac
1 teaspoon Dijon mustard

1. In a heatproof bowl, beat the egg yolks, yogurt, and lemon juice thoroughly.
2. Place the bowl over a pan of simmering water. Cook the sauce for 12 to 15 minutes, stirring frequently until it is thick.
3. Add all the spices and seasonings.
4. Stir well and pour into a sauce boat.

madznov-banri saltsa

CHEESE SAUCE

A family recipe. Serve with cooked eggs, pasta, or vegetables.

3 tablespoons (1½ oz/40 g) butter
3 tablespoons flour
¾ cup (200 ml) hot milk
¾ cup (200 ml) yogurt
1 teaspoon prepared strong mustard

4 oz (125 g) grated Gouda or
    Edam cheese
¼ teaspoon paprika
salt and pepper to taste

1. Melt butter in a saucepan and stir in the flour.
2. Cook for 1 minute.

3. Gradually add the milk and then the yogurt and cook slowly, stirring constantly, until thickened and smooth.
4. Mix in the cheese, mustard, paprika, salt, and pepper and cook slowly, stirring until the cheese melts.

tkemali sauce

PRUNE YOGURT SAUCE

This is a popular sauce from the Caucasus and is traditionally eaten with lamb or pork kebabs and *dapakhav madznov* (see p. 194).

½ lb (250 g) prunes
2 garlic cloves, crushed
¼ teaspoon salt
2 tablespoons finely chopped
   fresh cilantro

¼ teaspoon black pepper
1 tablespoon lemon juice
pinch of cayenne pepper
3 tablespoons yogurt

1. Wash the prunes and place in a saucepan with enough water to cover.
2. Bring to a boil and simmer for 10 to 15 minutes.
3. Strain the prunes into a sieve and reserve the liquid.
4. Leave the prunes until cool enough to handle and then remove and discard the pits.
5. Rub the prunes through a sieve and then dilute with some of the reserved liquid until the sauce has the consistency of thick cream.
6. Stir in the garlic, salt, black pepper, and cilantro.
7. Return the sauce to the pan and bring to a boil.
8. Stir in the lemon juice and cayenne pepper and remove from the heat.
9. Serve at room temperature; spoon the yogurt over the top and swirl into the sauce.

yogurtli toreotu sos

DILL YOGURT SAUCE

A recipe from Ismir in Turkey. Serve with cooked meat, poultry, or fish.

2 tablespoons (1 oz/25 g) butter
1 onion, finely chopped
2 tablespoons flour
salt and pepper to taste

2 cups (450 ml) hot chicken stock
juice of ½ lemon
generous ½ cup (150 ml) yogurt
2 tablespoons chopped fresh dill

1. Melt the butter in a saucepan and sauté the onion until it is soft and translucent.
2. Stir in the flour and cook for 1 minute, stirring constantly.
3. Season with salt and pepper.
4. Gradually add the hot stock and cook slowly, stirring constantly until it thickens.
5. Stir in the lemon juice, yogurt, and dill, and heat through, but do not boil.
6. Remove from the heat immediately.

yogurt cheese sauce

Try making cheese sauce with yogurt instead of milk. It is good with cooked eggs, vegetables, pasta, fish, or pancakes.

4 tablespoons (2 oz/50 g) butter
3 tablespoons flour
2 cups (450 ml) yogurt
½ teaspoon paprika

4 oz (100 g) grated cheese
   (Gouda, Edam, Cheddar, etc.)
½ teaspoon salt
dash of black pepper

1. Melt the butter in a saucepan.
2. Remove from the heat and stir in the flour.
3. Cook for 1 to 1½ minutes.
4. Beat the yogurt vigorously and gradually add to the pan.
5. Cook slowly and stir continuously until the sauce thickens.
6. Mix in the cheese, paprika, salt, and pepper.
7. Cook slowly until the cheese melts.

yogurt milkshake

You can make milkshakes with yogurt, using any kind of milkshake syrup, e.g. chocolate, pineapple, banana, vanilla. It makes an excellent drink.

SERVES TWO

¼ cup of the syrup of your
  choice
1 scoop of ice cream of the
  same flavor

1¼ cups (300 ml) milk
generous ½ cup (150 ml)
  plain yogurt

1. Put the ingredients in a blender and mix thoroughly.
2. Pour into two glasses.

lassi

This Indian version of *tan* or *dough* is the most popular drink on the Indian subcontinent. It is drunk in two ways, either sweet (*meetha*) or salted (*namkeen*). It is a perfect accompaniment for kebabs at a summer party.

SERVES SIX

2 cups (450 ml) yogurt
2 cups (450 ml) milk
juice of one lemon

½ teaspoon *kewra* extract (or
    substitute rosewater)
either sugar or salt to taste

1. In a large jug or mixing bowl, combine the yogurt, milk, lemon juice, and *kewra* extract or rosewater.
2. Stir well until the mixture is smooth.
3. Add the sugar or salt to taste and stir.
4. Pour into individual glasses and serve with some ice cubes and slices of lemon.

tan

This is a refreshing yogurt drink, popular throughout the Middle East. It is known as *ayran* or *laban* in Arabic-speaking lands, *dough* in Iran, and *tan* among Armenian-speaking people. It is an ideal accompaniment to kebabs and perfect as a summer drink. The proportions given here are for one person. They can be increased in proportion to the number required.

SERVES ONE

2 tablespoons yogurt
1¼ cups (300 ml) water
¼ teaspoon salt

¼ teaspoon dried mint
ice cubes

1. Spoon the yogurt into a glass and very gradually stir in the water to make a smooth mixture.
2. Stir in the salt and mint.
3. Drop in a few ice cubes and serve.

TAN WITH SODA WATER

In Iran, soda water is often used instead of plain water. It has a delightful flavor and the same quantities are used.

sweets and cakes

anoush-madzooni krema

SWEET YOGURT DRESSING

This recipe from the "old country" is usually added to fresh fruit salads or any fruit dessert. It is excellent with strawberries and makes an interesting change from cream.

1¼ cups (300 ml) yogurt
2 tablespoons honey (or ¼ cup superfine sugar)
1 tablespoon orange juice (or grape or pineapple juice)

½ teaspoon lemon juice
1 teaspoon grated lemon rind
pinch of salt
a few drops of rosewater

1. In a bowl, beat the yogurt until frothy.
2. Add the other ingredients.
3. Mix well.
4. Serve with fresh fruit salad, strawberries, or as a topping to any other fruit.

sweets & cakes

apple yogurt fool

An interesting new use of yogurt in an apple fool. Instead of cherries you can use any other candied fruit and angelica leaves for decoration.

SERVES FOUR

1 lb (½ kg) cooking apples
1 lemon rind
3 cloves

about 1 tablespoon brown sugar—
   the exact amount will depend on
   the apples and on individual taste
2 eggs, separated
generous ½ cup (150 ml) yogurt
candied cherries, to garnish

1. Peel, core, and slice the apples.
2. Place in a saucepan and add the lemon rind, cloves, and 2 tablespoons water.
3. Cover and simmer over low heat until the apples are soft.
4. Discard the lemon rind and cloves.
5. Put the apples and sugar in a blender or food processor and blend.
6. Return the purée to the saucepan.
7. Add the egg yolks to the apple purée and stir continuously on a low heat for 5 to 8 minutes, or until the egg yolks have thickened the purée.
8. Remove the pan from the heat, stir in the yogurt until thoroughly blended, and leave to cool.
9. Whisk the egg whites until stiff and fold into the cool apple purée.
10. Divide into individual dishes or pile into a serving dish and decorate with cherries.

apples with port

A lovely dessert that is simple and cheap to make. Use homemade yogurt to get the required consistency and that special flavor of home cooking.

1 lb (½ kg) cooking apples
4 tablespoons (2 oz/50 g) butter
4 oz (100 g) brown sugar
1 teaspoon cinnamon
a few drops of rosewater

⅓ cup (75 ml) port
generous ½ cup (150 ml) yogurt
1 tablespoon pistachio nuts,
    finely chopped

1. Peel and thickly slice the apples.
2. Melt the butter in a saucepan, add the apple slices, and cook, turning constantly, until soft and brown.
3. Add the sugar, cinnamon, rosewater, and port, and cook for a further 4 to 5 minutes. Taste and adjust if necessary.
4. Using a slotted spoon, transfer the apples to serving dishes.
5. Strain the sauce and pour onto the apples in each dish.
6. Spoon the yogurt over the apples, sprinkle with the pistachios, and serve.

apricot and yogurt custard

This tasty, attractive dessert is simple to prepare.

4 oz (100 g) dried apricots, soaked
  overnight in cold water
1¼ cups (300 ml) yogurt
2 egg yolks

1 tablespoon brown sugar
2 tablespoons chopped
  pistachio nuts

1. Preheat the oven to 325°F (160°C).
2. Cut the apricots into small pieces and put into a 4 cup (1 l) dish.
3. Beat the yogurt and egg yolks together and pour over the apricots.
4. Place the dish in a baking pan and pour enough cold water into the pan to come halfway up the dish.
5. Place in the oven and bake for 30 to 40 minutes until just set.
6. Mix the brown sugar and pistachio nuts together and sprinkle over the top.
7. Serve cold.

apricot and yogurt mousse

This delicious dessert, with its slightly tart flavor, is often welcome after a spicy or heavy main course. This recipe adapts easily to other fruits, such as raspberries, pears, strawberries, or blackcurrants.

1 tablespoon unflavored gelatin
  powder
3 tablespoons orange juice
1 large can (14–15 oz, 400–450 g)
  apricot halves
1 tablespoon sugar (optional)

1¼ cups (300 ml) yogurt
⅓ cup (75 ml) heavy whipping
  cream, whipped until stiff
1 oz (25 g) pistachio nuts, finely
  crushed or ground

1. Put the gelatin and orange juice in a small bowl and place over a saucepan of simmering water.
2. Stir until the gelatin dissolves and the mixture becomes clear.
3. Drain the apricot halves; place them in a blender with just sufficient orange juice to make a thick purée, and blend.
4. Empty the purée into a large bowl.
5. Stir in the gelatin mixture, sugar, yogurt, and whipped cream.
6. Turn the mixture into a wetted 4 cup (1 l) mold or serving dish and chill until firm.
7. If using a mold, turn the mousse out and sprinkle with the nuts.
8. Otherwise simply sprinkle the nuts over the mousse in the dish.
9. Serve immediately.

armeniaca

APRICOTS WITH YOGURT

This recipe was given to me by the chef of the Geghart restaurant in Armenia. It was created in honor of both the country and its fruit, the apricot (*Prunus armeniaca*). The recipe makes clever use of apricots.

1 lb (½ kg) apricots, pitted
  and halved
generous ½ cup (150 ml)
  apricot brandy
1¼ cups (8 oz/250 g) superfine sugar
4 tablespoons (2 oz/50 g) butter

4 eggs, separated
generous ½ cup (150 ml) yogurt
⅓ cup (75 ml) heavy cream
2 tablespoons pistachios, crushed

1. Preheat the oven to 350°F (180°C).
2. In a large saucepan, combine 2½ cups (600 ml) water, the apricots, and the brandy, and simmer over moderate heat until the apricots are nearly tender.
3. Using a slotted spoon, remove the fruit and set aside.
4. Add the sugar to the pan and raise the heat. Boil for 10 minutes until the water is reduced and the syrup has thickened.
5. Arrange the apricots in an ovenproof dish, dot with butter, and bake for 10 to 12 minutes.
6. Remove the dish from the oven, add the syrup, return to the oven, and cook for a further 15 minutes.
7. Remove the dish from the oven and allow to cool for 5 to 10 minutes.
8. Meanwhile, beat the egg yolks until fluid and add to the apricots.
9. Beat the egg whites until stiff and fold into the apricots; return the dish to the oven and bake for a further 12 to 15 minutes.
10. In a small bowl, beat the yogurt, cream, and pistachio together.
11. Pour over the apricots and serve immediately.

moz-bi-laban

BANANA YOGURT

A charmingly simple dessert from the Mediterranean coast, where very sweet bananas are grown. It is a childhood favorite.

2½ cups (600 ml) yogurt
4 ripe bananas

sugar to taste
1 teaspoon cinnamon

1. Pour the yogurt into a bowl and beat until creamy.
2. Thinly slice the bananas and very gently, stir them into the yogurt.
3. Stir in a little sugar at a time until it suits your taste.
4. Spoon into a large serving dish or into individual dishes, sprinkle with the cinnamon, and serve.

touz madznov

FIGS IN YOGURT

This dish is a Middle Eastern delicacy that my friends and I loved when we were young. We were able to pick the figs off the tree in our garden. It is extremely easy to make, but the fresh figs give it an exotic air. *Ser* or *kaymak* is the thick Middle Eastern cream that is normally cut with a knife. Clotted cream makes an excellent substitute if you can get it.

12 fresh figs
generous ½ cup (150 ml) *ser*
 or clotted or heavy cream

1¼ cups (300 ml) *anoush-madzooni
 krema* (see p. 259)
cinnamon
1 tablespoon pistachios

1. Drop the figs into a bowl of hot water, leave for 2 to 3 minutes, and then drain.
2. Peel off the skins and quarter the figs.

3. Whisk the cream a little and add to the yogurt sauce.
4. Spoon a little of the yogurt sauce into four to six serving glasses.
5. Divide the figs between the glasses and then spoon the remaining yogurt over the top.
6. Sprinkle with cinnamon and pistachios. Chill for at least an hour before serving.

mast ba hoolu

PEACHES WITH YOGURT

This is a simple dessert from Tehran, Iran, which is equally delicious hot or cold.

4 large, ripe peaches
2 tablespoons brown sugar
½ teaspoon ground cinnamon

1¼ cups (300 ml) stabilized yogurt (see p. 17)
¼ cup superfine sugar

1. Drop the peaches into boiling water for 10 seconds and then plunge them immediately into cold water.
2. Skin them, cut in half to remove the pits, and then slice.
3. Arrange the slices in four individual soufflé dishes.
4. Heat the broiler until it is red hot.
5. In a small dish, mix the brown sugar and cinnamon and sprinkle over the peaches.
6. Spoon the yogurt over the peaches.
7. Sprinkle each dish with 1 tablespoon of the sugar.
8. Place the dishes under the broiler and leave until the sugar melts and caramelizes.
9. Serve hot or cold.

fustukhe-wah-annanas

PINEAPPLE WITH YOGURT AND PISTACHIO NUTS

This is an unusual, highly successful combination, from Lebanon.

SERVES SIX

3 tablespoons self-rising flour
¼ cup superfine sugar
1 teaspoon baking soda
pinch of salt
4 eggs, separated

¼ pineapple, pulped and drained
1¼ cups (300 ml) yogurt
12 pineapple cubes (fresh or canned)
¼ cup chopped pistachios

1. Preheat the oven to 350°F (180°C).
2. In a bowl, mix the flour, sugar, baking soda, and salt.
3. In a small bowl, beat the egg yolks until they are lemon yellow.
4. Add the dry ingredients and the pulped pineapple and stir well.
5. Whisk the yogurt, add to the mixture, and stir until well blended.
6. Beat the egg whites until stiff and fold them gently into the mixture.
7. Pour the mixture into six ovenproof serving dishes.
8. Set the dishes in a shallow pan and pour sufficient cold water into the pan to come halfway up the dishes.
9. Place in the oven and bake for 45 to 60 minutes, or until the contents of the dishes are firm.
10. Meanwhile, roll the pineapple cubes in the chopped pistachios.
11. Garnish each dish with two of the pineapple cubes and serve.

nooranoush

POMEGRANATES AND YOGURT

This Armenian recipe is extremely attractive both in texture and color. It makes an excellent dessert.

scant 1 cup (175 g) superfine sugar
1 teaspoon lemon juice
¼ cup rosewater
2 large pomegranates
2 medium pomegranates
2 tablespoons clotted cream or
  heavy cream

2 tablespoons coarse dry
  breadcrumbs—or you could use
  crushed graham crackers instead
½ cup (120 ml) yogurt
2 tablespoons pistachios, chopped

1. First make the syrup: in a small saucepan, combine the sugar and lemon juice and 1¼ cups (300 ml) water.
2. Bring to a boil and simmer for 10 to 15 minutes, or until the syrup forms a film over the back of a spoon.
3. Stir in the rosewater and set aside.
4. Cut all the pomegranates in half and remove the seeds.
5. Retain the large pomegranate halves and remove any pith remaining in them.
6. Put the seeds and the breadcrumbs or crackers in a bowl, mix, and then mash.
7. Spoon the mixture into the pomegranate shells and pack tightly.
8. Pour the syrup slowly over the mixture, giving it time to soak through.
9. Place in the refrigerator and chill for 2 to 4 hours.
10. Whisk the yogurt and cream together and spoon over the pomegranates.
11. Sprinkle the chopped nuts over the top and serve immediately.

chocolate and nut cream

A delicious dessert with that tang which only yogurt can give.

2½ cups (600 ml) yogurt
5 tablespoons chocolate sauce
4 oz (100 g) small macaroons or
  amaretti cookies, crushed

4 oz (100 g) mixed nuts (e.g.
  walnuts, hazelnuts, almonds, and
  pistachios), roughly chopped

1. Pour the yogurt into a bowl, add the chocolate sauce, and stir well
   until you have a rippled effect.
2. Divide half the nuts and cookies between four glasses or sorbet dishes.
3. Spoon some of the yogurt mixture over the top.
4. Add the remaining cookies.
5. Spoon in the remaining yogurt mixture.
6. Top with the remaining nuts.
7. Chill in the refrigerator and serve.

fruit and nut yogurt pudding

A new and exciting recipe I found in a health magazine. I like it very much.

zest and juice of 1 orange
½ oz (15 g) unflavored gelatin
  powder
2½ cups (600 ml) yogurt
1 oz (25 g) brown sugar

1 oz (25 g) pitted dates, chopped
1 oz (25 g) walnuts or hazelnuts,
  finely chopped
1 oz (25 g) raisins
a few stewed apricots, to garnish

1. Pour the orange zest and juice into a small saucepan and sprinkle in
   the gelatin.

2. Place over low heat and allow to melt slowly and swell.
3. Pour the yogurt into a bowl, add the gelatin mixture and sugar, beat well to mix, and leave to cool.
4. When on the verge of setting, stir in the fruit and nuts.
6. Rub the inside of a 3–3½ cup (¾–1 l) jello mold with a few drops of oil.
7. Pour in the pudding and place in the refrigerator to set.
8. Turn the pudding on to a serving dish and garnish with a few stewed apricots.

yaourti me meli

YOGURT WITH HONEY

This is an unusual alternative to cream and is a beautiful accompaniment to desserts and cakes. Try it for breakfast. It is very popular throughout Greece.

generous ½ cup (150 ml) clear honey
1 teaspoon lemon zest
1 teaspoon orange zest
1 teaspoon white wine

1 teaspoon orange juice
½ teaspoon lemon juice
3 cups (¾ l) yogurt

1. Pour the honey into a mixing bowl and add the lemon and orange zests and the wine.
2. Beat until smooth.
3. Add the orange and lemon juice and whisk until frothy.
4. Add the yogurt and stir well.
5. Place in the refrigerator to chill.

ras gula

PANIR BALLS IN SYRUP

This is a great Indian sweet. If made well, these walnut-shaped balls of fresh
cheese, simmered in a syrup flavored with cardamom, are mouthwatering.

panir—made from 7¼ cups (1¾ l)
  milk and 3 tablespoons lemon
  juice (see p. 19)
3 teaspoons very fine semolina

about 12 sugar cubes
2 cups (500 g) sugar
6–8 cardamom pods, bruised
2–3 tablespoons rosewater

1. Empty the *panir* on to a work surface and knead with the heel of your hand for
   2 to 3 minutes.
2. Add the semolina and knead for a further 3 minutes until the cheese is
   smooth. When the palm of your hand becomes greasy, it is ready for molding.
3. Divide the mixture into about twelve walnut-sized balls.
4. Mold each one around a cube of sugar and roll into a ball between your palms.
5. Place the sugar and 4 cups (1 l) water in a large saucepan and bring slowly to a
   boil, stirring constantly until the sugar dissolves.
6. Simmer for 5 minutes.
7. Pour a quarter of the resulting syrup into a jug and set aside.
8. Add the cardamom pods and the cheese balls to the syrup remaining
   in the saucepan and bring to a boil.
9. Lower the heat and simmer until the balls swell and become spongy.
   This will take about 1 hour.
10. When the syrup thickens, add a little of the reserved syrup. Stir well.
11. Remove from the heat and stir in the rosewater.
12. Serve warm. They are very rich—serve only one or two per person to start
    with, spooning a little of the syrup over them.

smetanik

RUSSIAN RASPBERRY CHEESECAKE WITH YOGURT

This is a traditional Russian recipe, normally made with sour cream. I have tried it with yogurt instead and the result is beautiful. You can vary the fruit and use blueberries, blackberries, or strawberries instead. Use canned or frozen fruit if you like—you will find the results equally good.

1 lb (500 g) graham crackers or
   digestive biscuits, crushed
8 tablespoons (4 oz/125 g) butter,
   melted
½ teaspoon cinnamon
1¼ cups (300 g) cream cheese
1 egg
1¼ cups (300 ml) yogurt
¼ cup (50 g) superfine sugar

3 teaspoons lemon juice
¼ teaspoon salt

TOPPING
1 lb (½ kg) fresh or
   frozen raspberries
sugar to taste
1 tablespoon cornstarch
1 tablespoon lemon juice
¼ teaspoon cinnamon

1. Preheat the oven to 375°F (190°C).
2. Mix the crushed crackers or biscuits with the melted butter and the cinnamon and press evenly over the base of a 9 in (23 cm) round springform pan.
3. In a large mixing bowl, combine the cream cheese, egg, yogurt, superfine sugar, lemon juice, and salt.
4. Using an electric mixer, beat the ingredients together until smooth.
5. Spoon the mixture over the cracker or biscuit base.
6. Bake for approximately 40 to 45 minutes or until the center is almost set.
7. Remove from the oven and leave to cool.
8. Meanwhile, make the topping. Stew the fresh or frozen raspberries with about ⅓ cup (75 ml) water until just soft, but not reduced to a pulp. The fruit should be as intact as possible. Sweeten with sugar.
9. In a small saucepan, blend the cornstarch with a few tablespoons of the cool fruit syrup and then stir in the remaining syrup.

10. Bring to a boil, stirring constantly, and cook for about 3 minutes.
11. Remove from the heat and leave to cool.
12. Stir in the raspberries, lemon juice, and cinnamon.
13. Pour this raspberry topping over the cheesecake and chill for a few hours in the refrigerator.

awamaat

ARAB DOUGHNUTS

Doughnuts have been traditional fare in the Middle East for longer than in Europe. There are many variations. This recipe is from Syria. It does not use yeast or baking powder.

SYRUP
3 cups (750 g) sugar
2 teaspoons lemon juice
2 teaspoons rosewater

DOUGH
3⅔ cups (1 lb/500 g) self-rising flour
1 teaspoons baking soda
2 cups (450 ml) yogurt
3 cups (¾ l) vegetable oil
2 oz (50 g) finely chopped walnuts
    and pistachios, to garnish

1. Prepare the syrup: in a small pan, combine the sugar and lemon juice with 2½ cups (600 ml) water and bring to a boil.
2. Simmer until the syrup thickens and coats the back of the spoon.
3. Remove from the heat and stir in the rosewater. Keep hot.
4. Prepare the dough: sift the flour and baking soda into a large mixing bowl.
5. Gradually add the yogurt and knead well until you have a soft smooth dough.
6. Heat the oil in a large saucepan.
7. Break off small pieces of the dough and roll into balls about the size of marbles.
8. Drop a few at a time into the hot oil and deep fry, turning frequently, until they are golden brown all over.
9. Remove with a slotted spoon and drop into the hot syrup, stirring them around once or twice to make sure they are well coated.
10. Using a slotted spoon, transfer the doughnuts to a large plate.
11. Repeat until you have used all the dough.
12. Stack the doughnuts on a large serving plate, sprinkle with the nuts, and serve.

honey and ginger cheesecake

Simple, tasty cheesecake made of ginger snaps, honey, and yogurt.

BASE
8 oz (250 g) ginger snaps
8 tablespoons (4 oz/125 g) butter,
  melted

FILLING
1 cup (250 g) cream cheese
generous ½ cup (150 ml) yogurt

2 tablespoons honey
½ level tablespoon gelatin

DECORATION
⅓ cup (75 ml) heavy cream,
  whipped
pieces of crystallized ginger

1. Using a rolling pin or a blender, finely crush the ginger snaps.
2. Mix with the butter and press evenly over the base of an 8 in (20 cm) springform pan.
3. In a bowl, combine the cream cheese, yogurt, and honey and mix until smooth.
4. Place the gelatin with 2 tablespoons water into a small bowl over a saucepan of hot water and stir until the gelatin has dissolved and the mixture is clear.
5. Stir this into the cream cheese mixture.
6. Pour into the cake pan and leave to set.
7. Decorate with pieces of crystallized ginger and whipped cream.

jalebi

FRIED BATTER SWEETMEATS

This Indian sweet, perhaps one of the most eye-catching and popular, is very similar to one I remember tasting in the Middle East called *mushabek*. *Mushabek* is whirled around in beautiful circles. You can try making the *jalebi* in this way by using an pastry bag.

    To give them a brilliant orange color, add 1½ teaspoons of food coloring.

2⅔ cups (12 oz/350 g) all-purpose flour
½ oz (15 g) active dry yeast
generous ½ cup (150 ml) yogurt
1½ teaspoons orange food coloring
confectioner's sugar, for decoration
vegetable oil, for deep frying

SYRUP
2½ cups (1 lb/500 g) sugar
pinch of saffron
4 cloves
1 tablespoon rosewater

1. Sift flour into a large bowl, add the yeast and yogurt, and mix well. Gradually mix in sufficient warm water to form a batter.
2. If using, beat the food coloring into the batter.
3. Cover and let stand in a warm place for 3 to 4 hours.
4. Meanwhile, make the syrup: in a small saucepan, dissolve the sugar in 2½ cups (600 ml) water over low heat.
5. Stir in the saffron and cloves.
6. Bring to a boil and simmer until the syrup thickens.
7. Remove from the heat, add the rosewater, and set aside.
8. When the batter is ready, half-fill a deep frying pan or a large saucepan with vegetable oil. Heat until nearly boiling.
9. Using a pastry bag or a narrow funnel, allow the batter to run into the hot oil to form either the traditional figure eight, or double-circle whirls.
10. Fry, turning constantly for about 1 minute, until crisp and golden on both sides.
11. Lift out with a slotted spoon and drop into the syrup.
12. Let it soak for a few minutes—not more than 5 or it will get soggy—and transfer to a plate.
13. When all the *jalebi* are done, arrange them on a clean plate, dust with confectioner's sugar, and serve.

almond gingerbread

This cake has a fairly close texture and is generally quite moist. It should be baked as soon as the ingredients have been mixed together.

1¾ cups (8 oz/250 g) all-purpose flour
pinch of salt
2 teaspoons ground ginger
1 teaspoon baking soda
2 oz (50 g) ground almonds

½ cup (4 oz/100 g) margarine
⅓ cup (100 g) golden syrup
⅔ cup (100 g) soft brown sugar
generous ½ cup (150 ml) yogurt
1 egg, beaten
2 oz (50 g) slivered almonds

1. Preheat the oven to 325°F (160°C).
2. Line a 7 in (18 cm) square or 6½ in (16 cm) round cake pan with greased parchment paper.
3. Sift the flour, salt, ginger, and baking soda together into a bowl. Stir in the ground almonds.
4. Gently melt the margarine, syrup, and sugar in a pan over low heat.
5. Make a well in the center of the dry ingredients and pour in the syrup mixture. Add the yogurt and egg and beat until smooth.
6. Pour into the prepared pan. Scatter the almonds on top.
7. Bake in the center of the oven for 55 to 65 minutes or until the gingerbread is well risen and springy to touch.
8. Leave in the pan for 15 minutes; then turn out and cool on a wire rack.

banana gâteau

This is a delightful cake from Lebanon. The taste and aroma will speak for themselves. Eat soon as it will only keep for 2–3 days.

8 tablespoons (4 oz/100 g) butter, softened

4 oz (100 g) superfine sugar

2 eggs

pinch of salt

5 tablespoons yogurt

2 tablespoons rosewater

2 bananas, cut into thin slices

1¾ cups (8 oz/250 g) self-rising flour

½ teaspoon baking soda

1 oz (25 g) chopped almonds

confectioner's sugar

1. Cream the butter and sugar together until light and fluffy.
2. Break the eggs into a small bowl, add the salt, and whisk with a fork.
3. Beat the eggs into the butter-sugar mixture.
4. Beat in the yogurt and rosewater.
5. Add the banana slices and stir in very gently.
6. Sift the flour and baking soda into the mixture, add the almonds, and stir very gently until well blended.
7. Grease and flour a 7–7½ in (17–18 cm) round cake pan and spoon in the mixture.
8. Leave to rest for 30 minutes.
9. Preheat oven to 350°F (180°C).
10. Bake the cake for approximately 1 hour or until a knife inserted into the center comes out clean.
11. Leave to cool and then sift a little confectioner's sugar over the surface.

yogurtlu boregi

SWEET YOGURT PASTRIES

There are hundreds of recipes for making *boregi*—savory or sweet pastries using meat, vegetables, cheese, fruits, or nuts. This recipe uses yogurt and sugar and makes a wonderfully inexpensive and simple dessert.

3 egg yolks
½ teaspoon salt
2 tablespoons superfine sugar
5 tablespoons yogurt
2⅓ cups (10 oz/300 g) self-rising
   flour, sifted

oil for deep frying

GARNISH
superfine sugar or 4–5 tablespoons
   honey diluted with 1 tablespoon
   lemon juice

1. Put the egg yolks and salt in a large bowl and beat until a light lemony color.
2. Add the sugar and the yogurt and continue to beat.
3. Gradually fold in the flour; when the mixture thickens, knead to a dough.
4. Transfer to a lightly floured surface and continue kneading until the dough blisters.
5. Roll the pastry as thinly as possible.
6. Cut into ribbons about 1 in (3 cm) wide and then cut into strips 3 in (8 cm) long.
7. Tie each strip in a knot.
8. Heat the oil and cook a few pastries at a time until they are puffed up and golden. Turn just once.
9. Lift out with a slotted spoon and drain on paper towels.
10. Pile on to a serving plate and either sprinkle with superfine sugar or dilute the honey with the lemon juice and a little water and dribble over the pastries. Serve immediately.

yogurt tatlisi

This light sponge cake soaked in syrup is an adaptation of a well-known Turkish dessert. It is another recipe from Ifan Orga's *Cooking with Yogurt*. As this is rather a rich cake, I suggest that you serve it as an afternoon treat.

1 cup (250 ml) yogurt
3 cups (12 oz/350 g) confectioner's
   sugar
2 tablespoons melted butter
4 eggs, separated
2⅓ cups (10 oz/300 g) self-rising
   flour
½ teaspoon baking soda

GARNISH
whipped cream
pralined whole almonds (brown
   whole almonds evenly in the
   oven, sprinkling them frequently
   with confectioner's sugar. The
   heat caramelizes the sugar.)
2¼ cups (1 lb/450 g) superfine sugar
½ tablespoon lemon juice

1. Preheat the oven to 350°F (180°C).
2. Pour the yogurt into a mixing bowl and beat until creamy; stir in the confectioner's sugar and butter.
3. Beat the egg yolks until thick and stir into the yogurt mixture.
4. Sift the flour and baking soda together and fold into the batter.
5. Whisk the egg whites until stiff and fold gently into the sponge mixture.
6. Spoon into a greased and floured 8 in (20 cm) cake pan and bake for about 1 hour.
7. Meanwhile, make the syrup: in a saucepan, combine the sugar, 2½ cups (600 ml) water, and the lemon juice and bring to a boil.
8. Simmer for 7 to 10 minutes and remove from the heat.
9. When the cake is ready, remove it from the oven and pour the boiling syrup very slowly over it in the pan.
10. Leave to rest for about an hour, by which time all the syrup should have been absorbed.
11. Cut into small pieces and serve on individual plates topped with whipped cream and pralined almonds.

istanbul chocolate cake

This is a very popular cake among Turks and Armenians, and is cooked especially on festival days. This is an Armenian version, which uses brandy—most Turks, of course, do not use alcohol on religious grounds.

3 oz (75 g) dark chocolate
4 eggs, separated
¼ teaspoon salt
2 tablespoons (1 oz/25 g) butter
2 tablespoons vanilla extract or ¼
   cup (50 g) superfine sugar
1 cup (6 oz/150 g) self-rising flour
¼ teaspoon baking soda
⅓ cup (75 ml) yogurt
¼ cup (60 ml) brandy

FROSTING

6 oz (150 g) dark unsweetened
   chocolate, melted
2⅔ cup (12 oz/300 g) confectioner's
   sugar, sifted
2 tablespoons (1 oz/25 g) butter
1 oz (25 g) walnuts, finely chopped
brandy—enough to give the
   mixture a smooth consistency
crystallized violets

1. Preheat the oven to 350°F (180°C) and grease an 8 in (20 cm) round pan.
2. In a small, heatproof bowl, combine half of the chocolate with 1 tablespoon water. Place the bowl over a pan of hot water and stir well until the chocolate melts.
3. Beat the egg yolks with the salt.
4. Cream the butter and sugar together.
5. Beat in the egg yolks and melted chocolate.
6. Sift the flour and baking soda together and stir into the creamed mixture.
7. Stir in the yogurt and the brandy.
8. Beat the egg whites until stiff and fold gently into the cake mixture.
9. Pour into the prepared pan.
10. Bake for 45 to 50 minutes.
11. Turn on to a wire rack and cool.
12. Mix all the frosting ingredients together until you have a smooth consistency.
13. Cut horizontally through the middle of the cake.
14. Sandwich the two halves together using half the frosting.
15. Spread the remainder over the top and decorate with crystallized violets.

yaourtopita

YOGURT CAKE

A light, moist cake from Greece.

12 tablespoons (6 oz/175 g) butter
1¼ cups (8 oz/250 g) sugar
1 teaspoon lemon zest
4 eggs, separated
2 cups (10 oz/300 g) all-purpose flour

1 teaspoon baking powder
1 teaspoon baking soda
¼ teaspoon salt
½ cup (120 ml) yogurt
confectioner's sugar, to garnish

1. Preheat the oven to 350°F (180°C). Grease and flour an 8 in (18–20 cm) round cake pan.
2. In a large mixing bowl, combine the butter, sugar, and lemon zest and beat until light and fluffy.
3. Add the egg yolks and beat well.
4. Sift the flour, baking powder, baking soda, and salt together.
5. Add dry ingredients and yogurt alternately to the mixture.
6. Whisk the egg whites until stiff and fold gently into the cake mixture.
7. Pour quickly into the prepared pan.
8. Bake in the oven for about 1 hour or until the cake has shrunk away from the sides of the pan and is springy to the touch.
9. Turn onto a wire rack and cool.
10. Dust with confectioner's sugar before serving.

madzoonov mirtkatan

YOGURT FRUIT CAKE

This is an exceedingly rich cake from Gyumri, Armenia, full of the dried fruit of the region.

FRUIT MIXTURE
¼ lb (100 g) chopped figs
¼ lb (100 g) chopped dates
10 oz (300 g) raisins
2 oz (50 g) candied citrus peel
2 oz (50 g) chopped nuts
2 oz (50 g) chopped pistachio nuts
¼ cup (60 ml) orange juice
zest of ½ orange
2 tablespoons lemon juice
zest of ½ lemon

CAKE MIXTURE
1¼ cups (6 oz/175 g) self-rising flour
¼ teaspoon baking powder
½ teaspoon baking soda

¼ teaspoon salt
1 teaspoon cinnamon
¼ teaspoon ground nutmeg
¼ teaspoon ground cloves
4 tablespoons (2 oz/50 g) butter
2 tablespoons (50 g) margarine
½ cup (4 oz/100 g) granulated sugar
¼ cup (2 oz/50 g) brown sugar
2 large eggs
generous ½ cup (150 ml) yogurt
½ teaspoon vanilla extract
½ teaspoon almond extract
⅛ teaspoon lemon extract
(optional)
⅛ teaspoon orange extract
(optional)

1. Combine the fruit mixture ingredients and leave to stand overnight.
2. When ready to make the cake, preheat oven to 300°F (150°C) and grease a 9 in (23 cm) round cake pan. Flour only the base of the pan.
3. Sift together the flour, baking powder, baking soda, salt, cinnamon, nutmeg, and cloves, and set aside.
4. Cream the butter and margarine until soft and then beat in the brown and white sugars.

5. Blend in the eggs, yogurt, and extracts.

6. Add small amounts of the fruit mixture and flour mixture alternately to the creamed mixture and beat them in.

7. When all the ingredients are well blended, spoon the mixture into the greased baking pan, level with a knife, and place in the oven.

8. Bake for 1½ to 2 hours, until the blade of a knife inserted into the center comes out clean.

9. Turn the cake out to cool and then wrap it in foil. It tastes better if left to mature for a few days.

glossary

Besan Chickpea flour. Used extensively in Indian cuisine; available from most stores selling Asian food and many natural food stores.

Black cumin seeds (*Nigella sativa*) Known as *kala zeera* in India. This is not a true cumin; it has a different, more aromatic and peppery flavor.

Black mustard seeds (*Brassica nigra*) This variety is smaller and more pungent than the yellow variety; it is used in Indian, Middle Eastern, and Gulf regional cooking.

Bulgar Cracked wheat, steamed until partly cooked, dried, and then ground. It is available in fine, medium, or coarse grades—recipes specify which to use. Available in most Middle Eastern, Indian, and natural food stores.

Cilantro (*Coriandrum sativum*) A member of the parsley family. Both the leaves and seeds (known as coriander) of this plant are used in the Middle East. It has a pungent flavor somewhat similar to dried orange peel.

Feta Soft, crumbly white cheese made from goat's or ewe's milk.

Garam masala A spice mixture containing black pepper, cardamom, cinnamon, cloves, nutmeg, black cumin, coriander, and bay leaf. Can be purchased ready mixed from Indian grocery stores or online.

Ghee Pure butterfat. Ghee can be heated to a high temperature without burning. It is superior to ordinary butter and has a fragrance of its own. Used extensively in Indian and Middle Eastern cooking. Available in all Indian and Middle Eastern stores. *Samna* in Arabic.

Halloumi A salty sheep's milk cheese, which is matured in whey. Sometimes flavored with mint or black cumin.

Kaymak or Ser A thick cream that can literally be cut with a knife; usually prepared with buffalo's milk. The nearest substitute is thick clotted cream.

Kewra A variety of screwpine (*Pandanus odoratissimus*). Mostly used for flavoring Indian sweets. Can be bought as an essence or concentrate. It is strong; one drop is usually enough.

Polenta Cornmeal (maize flour) dried in the open, not in the oven. Can be purchased from Italian and Balkan food stores and most grocery stores.

Sumac (*Rhus corioria*) The dried, crushed red berries of a species of the sumac tree. It has a sour, lemony taste. Crush and steep it in water to extract its essence, which can then be used in stews instead of lemon juice.

Tahina An oily paste made from toasted sesame seeds. If left standing it tends to separate and needs to be blended before use. Available in all Middle Eastern stores and natural food stores.

Tourshi Pickles, a must on any Middle Eastern dinner table. Small cucumbers, chili peppers, carrots, eggplants, cauliflowers, etc., are home pickled and often served as the only accompaniment to a meat dish.

index